The Secrets of Ancient Egypt

Egyptian Pyramids and the Secrets of the Pharaohs

Federico Puigdevall and Albert Cañagueral

Cavendish Square

New York

This edition published in 2018 by Cavendish Square Publishing, LLC
243 5th Avenue, Suite 136, New York, NY 10016

First Edition

Website: cavendishsq.com

Cataloging-in-Publication Data

Names: Puigdevall, Federico, 1955-. | Cañagueral, Albert.
Title: The secrets of ancient Egypt / Federico Puigdevall and Albert Cañagueral.
Description: New York : Cavendish Square Publishing, 2018. | Series: The secrets of history | Includes bibliographical references and index.
Identifiers: ISBN 9781502632654 (library bound)
Subjects: LCSH: Egypt--Civilization--To 332 B.C.--Juvenile literature.Egypt--Antiquities--Juvenile literature.
Classification: LCC DT61.P85 2018 | DDC 932/.01--dc23

Editorial Director: David McNamara
Editor: Erica Grove
Associate Art Director: Amy Greenan
Production Coordinator: Karol Szymczuk

Original Idea Sol90 Publishing
Project Management Nuria Cicero
Editorial Coordination Diana Malizia
Editorial Team Alberto Hernández, Virginia Iris Fernández, Mar Valls, Marta de la Serna, Sebastián Romeu. Maximiliano Ludueña, Carlos Bodyad-
jan, Doris Elsa Bustamante, Tania Domenicucci, Andrea Giacobone, Constanza Guariglia, Joaquín Hidalgo, Hernán López Winne.
Proofreaders Marta Kordon, Edgardo D'Elio
Design Fabián Cassan
Layout Laura Ocampo, Carolina Berdiñas, Clara Miralles, Paola Fornasaro, Mariana Marx, Pablo Alarcón

The photographs in this book are used by permission and through the courtesy of: Album; Getty Images; Cordon Press; Corbis/Cordon Press; Age
Fotostock; National Geographic Stock; Topfoto, Granger, Other Images; Alamy; HolyLandPhotos (www.HolyLandPhotos.org); John M. Allegro,
Allegro Estate; Israel Antiquities Authority, Clara Amit; Photos © The Israel Museum, Jerusalem.

Printed in the United States of America

A Genuine Architectural Feat

The Pyramids: Symbols of Eternal Life

How Were the Pyramids Built?

Were They Built by Slaves?

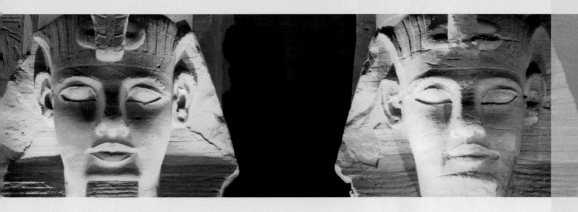

A Genuine Architectural Feat

The step pyramid of Zoser in Saqqara—the work of Imhotep, master in the art of building during the third dynasty of Egypt—was the first Egyptian monument built of stone. It paved the way for a period of advancement in science, knowledge, and technical progress during the fourth dynasty, known as "the century of the pyramids." From the pyramid of Meidum to the second pyramid of Giza, great advances take place that are credited to a single royal family: Snefru, the father; Khufu (Cheops, in Greek), the son, and Khafra (Chephren, in Greek), the grandson. Under the reign of these pharaohs, close to twenty million tons of stone were extracted, transported, and placed in monuments of perfect pyramidical form; works that today we call "pharaonic." With the advent of the smooth-sided pyramid, this era would be marked by technical experimentation that resulted in the Great Pyramid of Khufu, a masterpiece of architecture and engineering. The pyramid of Khafra would mark the end of the enormous funerary monuments, and the pyramid for his son Menkaure (Mycerinus, in Greek) would initiate a new era of smaller monuments, where writings would later appear.

History kept silent regarding the techniques that were used for the construction of the pyramids, which left the door open to numerous theories. The most significant ones are grouped into two separate branches. The view of the "machinists" has no archaeological basis, but is rooted in descriptions by the Greek historian Herodotus, who visited the plateau of Giza two thousand years before the works were finished. The other view, of the "ramp builders," proposes two options: the use of a straight front ramp—that would need as much material for its construction as for the pyramid itself—or a zig-zag ramp, going up the sides of the monument. Those that uphold this last Hypotheses are uncertain of how the ramps would have maintained stability and duration, and in the case of the pyramid of Khufu, borne the transport of the granite beams of up to 60 tons (54.4 mt).

The reason that both proposals fail is narrow thinking, based on an incorrect premise: that the pyramids were constructed from the outside. From that basis, no solution could be verified. The key factors in the smooth-sided pyramids are two inseparable elements: the corbelled vault, which allowed the construction of chambers, passages, or tunnels that could withstand enormous loads; and limestone from Tura, used in facades, which made possible the construction of perfect pyramids thanks to its fineness, whiteness, and beauty. The original delicacy of this stone is lost upon contact with the atmosphere, which made it easy to extract, carve, and carry from the quarry.

It was only possible to erect the pyramids by first placing these blocks of facade as the construction progressed, level by level, from the base to the top. The only solution was to build the monument from the inside. At the beginning, and during up to two-thirds of the total work, materials would have been delivered for the construction through a short front ramp outside. Later, the delivering of supplies toward the peak would have taken place by means of an interior tunnel ramp, covered by a corbelled vault, that had been built within the monument at the beginning of the operation. Using the artistry of measurement, the Egyptians could retrieve materials from the outside ramp and bring them through the inner ramp to build the remaining top portion of the pyramid.

Progress in engineering allowed the architectural feat that is the pyramid of Khufu: a burial chamber covered with a flat roof within the heart of the monument. The construction of a great pyramid had a religious purpose: to ensure the king's eternity in the afterlife. The pyramidical shape, perfectly oriented toward the cardinal points and therefore witness to the journey of the Sun, represented the eternal cycle of the life and death of the king during the day and night.

Jean-Pierre Houdin

French Architect. Studied at the École des Beaux-Arts of Paris. In 2008 he published *The Secret of the Great Pyramid: How One Man's Obsession Led to the Solution of Ancient Egypt's Greatest Mystery*, in which he tackles the mystery of the construction of the pyramids.

THE JEWELS OF GIZA
The pyramids of the Pharaohs
Khufa (*right*) and Khafra (*left*)
rise behind the Great Sphinx
of Giza.

The Pyramids: Symbols of Eternal Life

More than 4,500 years after their construction, the pyramids of Egypt continue to defy imagination. How were they built? Who erected them? What exactly was their purpose?

A sacred river splits the land in two. It runs from south to north, and ends in the sea, blossoming out like a lotus flower. The Land of the Living is found on its east bank, where the Sun God Ra (whom the ancient Egyptians associated with Atum, the primordial god, and also with Horus) comes into the world each day. On the west bank, where after the passing of each day the Sun is swallowed by Nut (Goddess of the Sky), is the Land of the Dead, the resting place of the departed. The ancient Egyptians thought of the course of the Sun as Ra's ship crossing the ocean of the sky. Ra was conceived again during the night to be reborn in the early hours of the morning.

Since the dawn of history, the Egyptians attributed divine origin and nature to their kings. To them, the Pharaoh was the incarnation of Horus on earth, the god-king. And, like a god, the Pharaoh had a more sublime destiny than other mortals: after his life on earth, he was entitled to a "celestial" existence. Purified by the water of a mythical lake, the Pharaoh had a place in the solar ship and made the daily journey through the sky's ocean at Ra's side. Although we know quite a bit about the origins of Egyptian civilization, experts do not all agree when it comes to defining the different ages and periods of its history, and different timeframes are given with differences that range from 50 to 200 years depending on the theory. However, there is data on the details and routines of

daily Egyptian life, as well as of their social organization, customs, and beliefs, based on the painted murals and the texts discovered by scholars and researchers of the Old Kingdom (2686-2134 BCE), a period of more than half a millennium during which the third (III) to sixth (VI) dynasties reigned, and during which the most magnificent pyramids were built. It was during this era that the Great Pyramid of Giza (the tomb of Khufu) was erected in the outskirts of Cairo. It is the only one of the seven wonders of the ancient world that is still standing. It was also during this era that the myth of a god intimately connected with funeral rites, and by extension with the pyramids, might have taken shape: Osiris, considered the prototype of the deceased kings. Elevated to the rank of Ruler

KHAFRA'S PYRAMID
It is a part of the Giza Necropolis.
It is located near the pyramid of
Khufu, from whose top this pic-
ture was taken.

of the Country of the Blessed, Osiris represents royalty, accounts for the continuity of the monarchy, and is connected with the myth of the deceased king who dies transmitting his dignity to his son Horus and rises again in a beatified form.

We are not sure whether the pyramids were only meant to be royal tombs or also a resting place for the pharaohs' souls (ka), but we do know that all the kings who sat on the throne of Egypt were considered to successively pass through these two states: vested with the dignity of Horus during their reign, they would transform into Osiris at the end of their life and were honored as such by their sons and successors. There is no doubt that the pyramids were part of the complex plethora of religious rituals surrounding the Pharaohs and their journey to the afterlife. That sort of certainty is rare amid the many questions that are still raised by these wonderful structures, which challenge science and are a fertile field for the most fantastic speculations. Proof has been found of at least 120 of these spectacular works of architecture remaining today, all located on the western side of the Nile Valley, in the Land of the Dead. Although they are associated with the entire Egyptian civilization, they are characteristic of a single time period: The Old Kingdom.

Under subsequent rules, during what is known as the Middle Kingdom (approximately between 2030 BCE and 1640 BCE) the pyramids decreased in size and quality.

And in the New Kingdom, they only appear as external elements of some artisan tombs. However, the three on the plains of Giza, named Khufu, Khafra, and Menkaure (in Greek Cheops, Chephren, and Mykerinos, respectively), have become a symbol of ancient Egypt and are an ongoing subject of fascination caused by a culture as sophisticated as it is enigmatic. Most notable is the first and largest of them, the construction of which was ordered by the Pharaoh Khufu around 2580 BCE, and which would have been erected by his architect, Hemiunu.

ADMIRED BY GREECE AND ROME

Aristotle referred to the pyramids in his *Politics*, pointing out that they would have served to keep the population busy and prevent plots against the Pharaohs. Meanwhile, Herodotus gives a detailed description of the pyramids and the method used to construct them, which he attributes to slaves using pulleys and rudimentary machines, although some researchers argue that the so-called "Father of History" may not have traveled to Egypt and only based his writings on the many stories and legends in circulation during his time, the fifth century BCE. The Giza Pyramids were already 2,000 years old at that time.

The Romans also had a great fascination with Egypt and its pyramids. Besides incorporating a number of Egyptian myths and deities into their culture, such as the

NECROPOLIS
The pyramids of Giza and the Great Sphinx are the most visible monuments of a necropolis that also included other cemeteries, as well as homes and workshops for the workers who built them.

HIEROGLYPHS
The writing system of the Egyptians was based on a combination of phonetic and ideographic principles. After several years of research, the Frenchman Jean-Francois Champollion was able to decipher it in 1823.

goddess Isis, several generations of Roman aristocracy used pyramids to mark their own graves during the first centuries of Christianity. Some Roman emperors even came to consider themselves true Pharaohs. They took all sorts of objects from the Nile region to Rome, which contributed to the spread of Egyptian aesthetic sensibilities among the elites of the Eternal City. They also imported a good amount of scientific knowledge regarding medicine, mathematics, and astronomy, as well as religious rituals and many

of the customs of the upper classes and priesthood. In medieval Christian tradition, it was considered that the pyramids were granaries built by the patriarch Joseph spoken of in the Bible. It wasn't until the Renaissance that debates began among scholars regarding the construction and possible purpose of the pyramids. At this time legends began to spread about fantastic treasures hidden inside them and about the spirits that inhabited them. In the Arab world of that time, which was not considered heir to these struc-

tures, there had already been much talk about the presence of strange rooms in the depths of the pyramids, as well as the mysterious secrets they held.
During the Romantic era, and specifically while the Orientalist movement swept through Europe in the nineteenth century, when communication was opened between East and West, the basis of what would later be called Egyptology was established.
Napoleon's expedition to Egypt in 1798, with the intention of preventing access to

Continued on page 18 ▶

Prominent Pyramids

They are the most important architectural creation of Ancient Empire, and a fundamental part of the architectural collection devoted to the worship of the Pharaohs. While their primary purpose was to serve as funerary monuments, many were never used as tombs.

Plains of Giza

While Egypt has at least 120 pyramids, the ones in Giza are undoubtedly the most famous, due to their size and the quality of the construction.

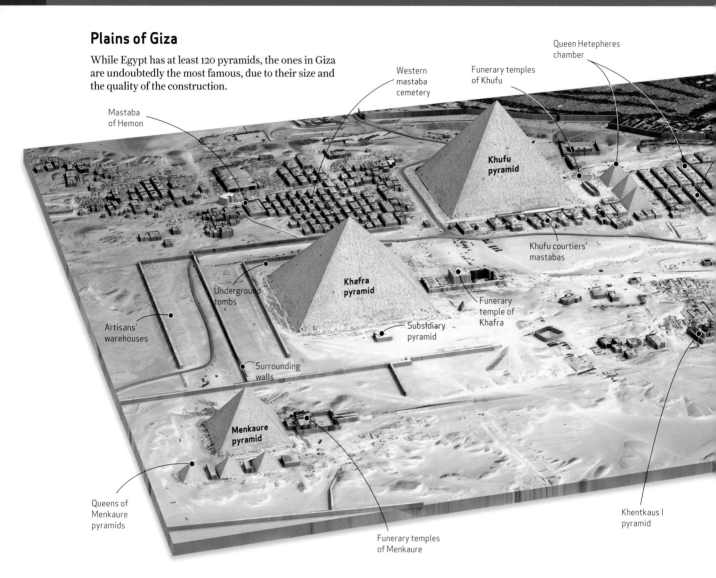

Mastaba of Hemon

Western mastaba cemetery

Funerary temples of Khufu

Queen Hetepheres chamber

Khufu pyramid

Khufu courtiers' mastabas

Underground tombs

Khafra pyramid

Funerary temple of Khafra

Artisans' warehouses

Subsidiary pyramid

Surrounding walls

Menkaure pyramid

Queens of Menkaure pyramids

Khentkaus I pyramid

Funerary temples of Menkaure

Chronology of the Building of the Major Pyramids

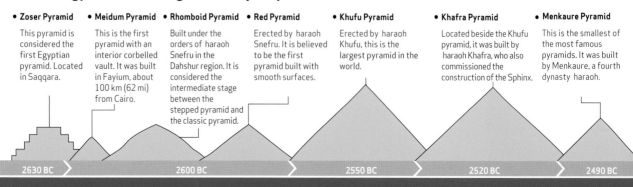

- **Zoser Pyramid**

  This pyramid is considered the first Egyptian pyramid. Located in Saqqara.

- **Meidum Pyramid**

  This is the first pyramid with an interior corbelled vault. It was built in Fayium, about 100 km (62 mi) from Cairo.

- **Rhomboid Pyramid**

  Built under the orders of haraoh Snefru in the Dahshur region. It is considered the intermediate stage between the stepped pyramid and the classic pyramid.

- **Red Pyramid**

  Erected by haraoh Snefru. It is believed to be the first pyramid built with smooth surfaces.

- **Khufu Pyramid**

  Erected by haraoh Khufu, this is the largest pyramid in the world.

- **Khafra Pyramid**

  Located beside the Khufu pyramid, it was built by haraoh Khafra, who also commissioned the construction of the Sphinx.

- **Menkaure Pyramid**

  This is the smallest of the most famous pyramids. It was built by Menkaure, a fourth dynasty haraoh.

2630 BC   2600 BC   2550 BC   2520 BC   2490 BC

nigmas

How Long Did It Take to Build a Pyramid?

According to the data obtained, Hemiunu, the architect who directed the construction at Giza, spent almost two years planning the works. There was a schedule set for the tasks, according to the seasons, for each activity as permitted by religion. According to this plan, the first thousand days were spent placing the first line of masonry. The next thousand days were spent in finishing the king's chamber, and a thousand days later the pyramid was finished.

Map of Egyptian Pyramids

All the Egyptian pyramids are located along the western bank of the Nile, "the land of the dead," and are close to towns, probably because they needed an infrastructure for the complex building.

Eastern mastaba cemetery

Great Sphinx

Temple of the Sphinx

Enlarged area

Valley funerary temple of Khafra

Abu Rawash

Giza • Cairo

Zawyet el-Arian

Abusir

Saqqara

LOWER EGYPT

Dahshur

Mazghuna

El-Lisht

Meidum

Sila

Hawara

El-Lahun

Eastern Desert

PYRAMID TYPES

There are three types of pyramid shapes in Egypt:

Stepped Pyramid

This pyramid is made up of six mastabas, one on top of the other, decreasing in size towards the top.

Rhomboid Pyramid

Features a double inclination. This could be due to a mistake in calculations that would have ended in collapse if the original design was followed.

Smooth Pyramid

Smooth pyramid with square base that becomes proportionally smaller towards the top.

Red Sea

Western Desert

Nile River

• **Pepi II Pyramid**

It was erected in Saqqara by the last pharaoh of the sixth dynasty. Contains texts that provide valuable information about pharaonic Egypt.

2278 BC

UPPER EGYPT

The oldest royal cemetery of Egypt is located in Abidos.

Valley of the Kings

Britain's trade routes to India, was decisive in this issue.

With more than 50,000 men and 154 scientists aboard 300 ships, the Emperor of France landed in Alexandria on July 2 of that year. Just twenty days later, he defeated the Turks in the Battle of the Pyramids, and just a month later, on August 22, he founded the Institute of Egypt in Cairo.

In September, French scientists were already working in the Giza plains. Among them were the mathematician Gaspard Monge and the chemist Claude Louis Berthollet, who were both over 50 years old and already renowned scholars when set out for Egypt, while most of their colleagues were younger than 30. Recruited by teachers and friends, many would become famous. This was the case with Dominique Vivant Denon, author of the book *Journey in Lower and Upper Egypt*, in which he chronicles his journey down the Nile between January and March of 1799. Denon discovered Thebes, Karnak, Luxor and Aswan for the West. He became director of several French museums including the Louvre. Many current Egyptologists believe his book to be the starting point that indicates the date of birth of Egyptology. Others, however, consider it just another travel book written in late eighteenth-century Europe.

Of those who collaborated with Napoleon, two others would also become famous: Nicolas Jacques Conté, inventor of pencil lead, and Etienne Geoffroy Saint-Hilaire, a distinguished professor of zoology. Napoleon drew together the labors of all his collaborators into a monumental work, *Description of Egypt*, which was fundamental to the knowledge and spread of the Nile country's culture, and which constituted a definitive step forward in understanding the history and lives of the pyramid builders.

At that time it was understood that the pyramids had a single function, which was exclusively funerary, and they were identified with a society completely enslaved by the despotic power of the Pharaohs. That idea continued to be the understanding during much of the twentieth century.

Today we know that this was not exactly true, thanks to the work of many archaeologists, explorers, and travelers who dedicated themselves to this topic from the eighteenth century to the present.

THE LEADING RESEARCHERS

Among the most notable scholars, we can cite Heinrich Menu von Minutoli (1772–1846), the Prussian general who explored the country between 1820 and 1821; John Shae Perring (1813–1869), the English Egyptologist who studied the pyramid of Menkaure with Richard William Howard Vyse; Alexander Badawy (1913–1986), Egyptian-born and author of one of the most important histories of Egyptian architecture published to this day; and Jean-Philippe Lauer (1902–2001) French architect and archaeologist who spent 70 years in Egypt, considered the foremost expert in pyramid construction techniques and methods. Lauer worked at Saqqara from 1926 until his death in 2001.

The most important figure in this field in recent years is undoubtedly Mark Lehner, an American researcher considered a living legend of modern Egyptology, creator of a computerized reconstruction of the Great Sphinx of Giza and of a series of important works on the Great Pyramid.

Zahi Hawass also stands out as one of the world's most famous Egyptologists. He served as secretary general of the Supreme Council of Antiquities of the Egyptian government. To both of these men, the pyramids are not just memorials but rather one more element of a complex architectural ensemble used in the practice of a great number of rituals and that fulfilled an important role in binding the community life of

Zahi Hawass
1947

One of the brightest Egyptologists today. He had a degree in Greek and Roman archaeology at the age of 19. Starting in 2002, he served as secretary general of the Supreme Council of Antiquities of Egypt, a post he left in late 2009 when he was appointed deputy minister of culture. Among his most resounding discoveries are the identification of the mummy of Hatshepsut and the discovery of new passages in the Great Pyramid. He also directed the computerized tomography performed on the mummy of Tutankhamen in 2005.

DEDICATION Hawass has worked hard to bring the treasures of Ancient Egypt, dispersed throughout the world, back to their country of origin.

John Shae Perring
1813–1869

British engineer who investigated the pyramid of Dahshur along with Richard William Howard Vyse. In 1837, using explosives, he entered the pyramid of Menkaure and discovered an empty sarcophagus and a large mummified bird. A sketch he drew shows the exterior of the tomb with lines outlining its inner chambers.

DAHSHUR Perring made the first truly scientific exploration of the pyramid of Dahshur, known as the bent pyramid, in 1839.

◀ *Continued from page 15*

Mark Lehner

American archaeologist and Egyptologist, with a Doctorate in Egyptology from Yale University (1990), Mark Lehner is also a professor of Egyptian archeology at the Oriental Institute of the University of Chicago and a Research Associate at the Semitic Museum at Harvard University. From 1979 to 1983 he directed the Sphinx and Isis Temple project. Since 1984 he has been director of the Giza Plateau Mapping Project. He worked on the tomb of Khufu and that of his mother (the Queen Mother). Thanks to his work at Giza, abundant archaeological remains of what appear to be the homes and workshops of the laborers that would have worked as the builders of the pyramids were discovered, as well as a huge cemetery with graves and remains of hundreds of people buried beside the pyramids. His book, *The Complete Pyramids* (1997), is considered a classic of Egyptology.

CONTRIBUTIONS TO GIZA Along with Zahi Hawass, Mark Lehner discovered the importance of the town found on the plain of Giza, which they both identified as the "city of the builders" of the surrounding pyramids.

1950

"From all indications, it was not slaves who carried out the task of building the pyramids, but rather workers from different parts of Egypt." M. L.

Jean Philippe Lauer

1902–2001

The most famous of French Egyptologists dedicated almost his entire life to the study of the ancient Nile culture, a commitment that began in the heyday of the excavations in Egypt and continued until the twenty-first century, when he passed away at 99. Much of his work was devoted to the restoration of the pyramid of Saqqara. He restored the limestone walls of the enclosure of Zoser's funerary complex, built around the famous "step" pyramid, block by block for seventy years.

WORKS Lauer excavated the funerary complex of Zoser and restored the room known as the blue ceramic room. He also reconstructed part of Zoser's Temple of Ka ("life force").

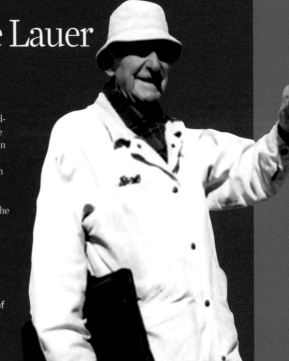

Great Pyramid of Giza

Pharaoh Khufu ordered the building of the Great Pyramid around 2550 BCE. It was located at the center of a group of religious buildings, some of which do not exist anymore, like the funerary temple and the Valley Temple. While its entrance was hidden, it was plundered by 2150 BCE.

A Monumental Work

About 4,000 men – quarry workers, carriers, and builders – worked for almost 30 years building this pyramid that, when finished, weighed six million tons.

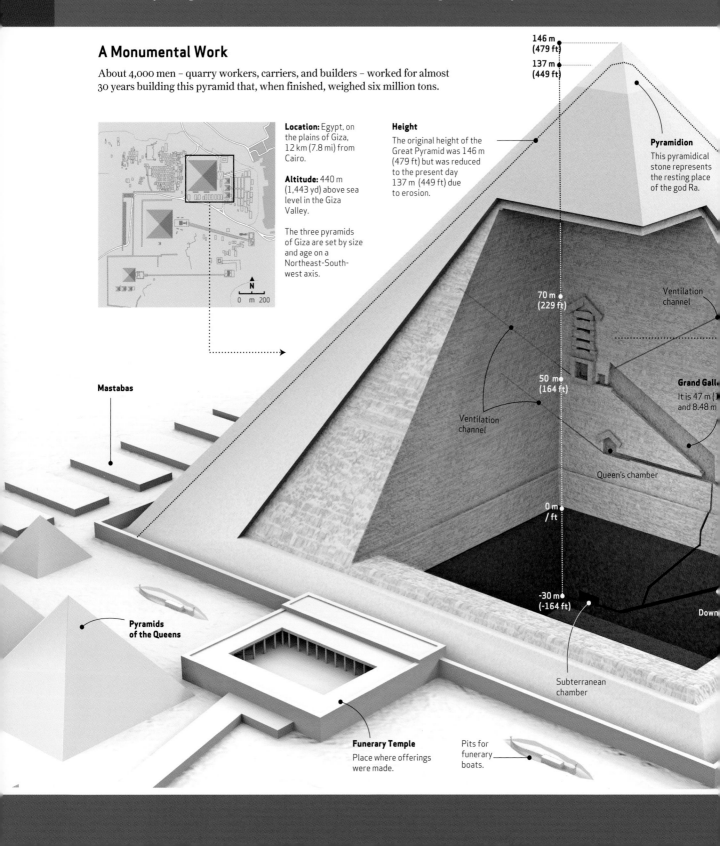

Location: Egypt, on the plains of Giza, 12 km (7.8 mi) from Cairo.

Altitude: 440 m (1,443 yd) above sea level in the Giza Valley.

The three pyramids of Giza are set by size and age on a Northeast-Southwest axis.

N
0 m 200

Height

The original height of the Great Pyramid was 146 m (479 ft) but was reduced to the present day 137 m (449 ft) due to erosion.

Pyramidion
This pyramidical stone represents the resting place of the god Ra.

146 m (479 ft)

137 m (449 ft)

70 m (229 ft)

50 m (164 ft)

0 m / ft

-30 m (-164 ft)

Ventilation channel

Ventilation channel

Grand Gall...
It is 47 m (and 8.48 m

Queen's chamber

Down...

Mastabas

Pyramids of the Queens

Subterranean chamber

Funerary Temple
Place where offerings were made.

Pits for funerary boats.

nigmas

How Was the Construction of the Great Pyramid Organized?

There is no certainty about the kind of organization used. According to the analysis of archaeologist Mark Lehner, they would have set up a construction camp in the Giza plain that had the essential raw material, limestone, and established a harbor by the Nile shore close to the construction spot. Roads would link the entrance with the quarry and the building location. The appearance of the site is unknown because it was buried by a town close to Giza.

Height

This was the world's highest building until the construction of the Eiffel tower in 1889.

The original outer layer was made of fine white limestone which reflected the sunlight.

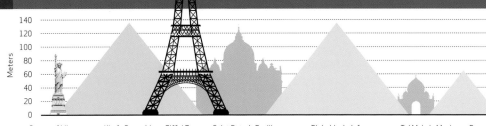

| | Statue of Liberty USA 93 m (305 ft) 1886 | Khufu Pyramid Egypt 137 m (449 ft) 2550 BCE | Eiffel Tower France 324 m (1,062 ft) 1889 | Saint Peter's Basilica Vatican 132 m (433 ft) 1626 | Pirámide de Jafra Egipto 136 m (446 ft) 2520 BCE | Taj Mahal India 60 m (196 ft) 1654 | Menkaure Pyramid Egypt 65.5 m (214.1 ft) 2490 BCE |

The Great Pyramid is made up of 2,300,000 stone blocks, each with an average weight of 2.5 tons, although there were bigger blocks.

KING'S CHAMBER

This was the final resting place for Pharaoh Khufu, made of granite. The roof is made of stones that weight 50 tons each. It also has relieving chambers, probably to reduce the pressure of the enormous weight of the stone structure above.

Hieroglyphs

Ventilation channel

Enlarged area

Granite horizontal beams

Limestone support beams

Relieving chambers

Entrance

Sarcophagus

Ventilation channel

230 m (754.7 ft)

King's chamber

King's chamber entrance

Antechamber

Main Gallery

Surrounding wall

The large platform upon which the monumental building was built measures 1,500 m (4,921 ft) North to South and 2,000 m (6,561 ft) East to West.

HIEROGLYPHS

Some relieving chambers above the King's chamber have hieroglyphs. This is the only place in the whole pyramid where the name of Pharaoh Khufu appears.

KHUFU

The Cities of the Pyramids

Life around the pyramids did not end with the completion of the works and the burial of the Pharaoh. Cities were also erected specifically so that a group of officials of ancient Egypt could move in and oversee the work.

These officials generally controlled the accounting of the works, but their permanent residence was most likely elsewhere. Scribes, priests, and other people lived in adobe buildings built around the pyramids, along with the rest of the people who were involved in the construction. All this activity was documented on papyrus. In Giza, east of the pyramid of Menkaure, the remains of one of these transient cities was found by chance.

Moreover, after completion of the work, the Egyptian authorities faced the same problem that all states that promoted the construction of giant works had to solve: maintenance.

Towards the end of the Old Kingdom, Egypt had 20 pyramids with their respective temples, constructed with varying degrees of strength. According to estimates by scholars like Barry Kemp, a renowned professor of Egyptology at the University of Cambridge, there was no established maintenance policy. Over the years, each Pharaoh devoted more or less effort to restoring the works that were damaged, according to his own discretion.

According to the information available, at the time of the New Kingdom a general policy was consolidated on replacing the old temples, ruined by the passage of time, by others constructed with more solid materials.

PYRAMID OF MENKAURE
In excavations conducted around this pyramid, traces of a small town adjoining the tomb of Queen Khentkaus were found.

Sculptures of Amazing Quality

At different stages, archaeologists found dust-covered sculptures of great historical and artistic value buried in rubble by the pyramid of Menkaure. Examples are the slate triad showing the monarch accompanied by two other figures, considered one of the highest quality works of all those made by the sculptors of the Old Kingdom. Slabs of alabaster were also found, as well as some diorite statues which were probably objects of worship for the Egyptians during their time.

TRIAD OF MENKAURE
Represents the Pharaoh Menkaure, the goddess Hathor, and the nome of Upper Egypt.

an entire culture around the worship of a Pharaoh-god. Considered by some researchers as the culmination of scientific and philosophical progress that dates back to the early Neolithic period of Pharaonic culture and that developed for thousands of years, the pyramids were also, when built, a symbol of eternal life and regeneration. It is telling

◀ Continued from page 18

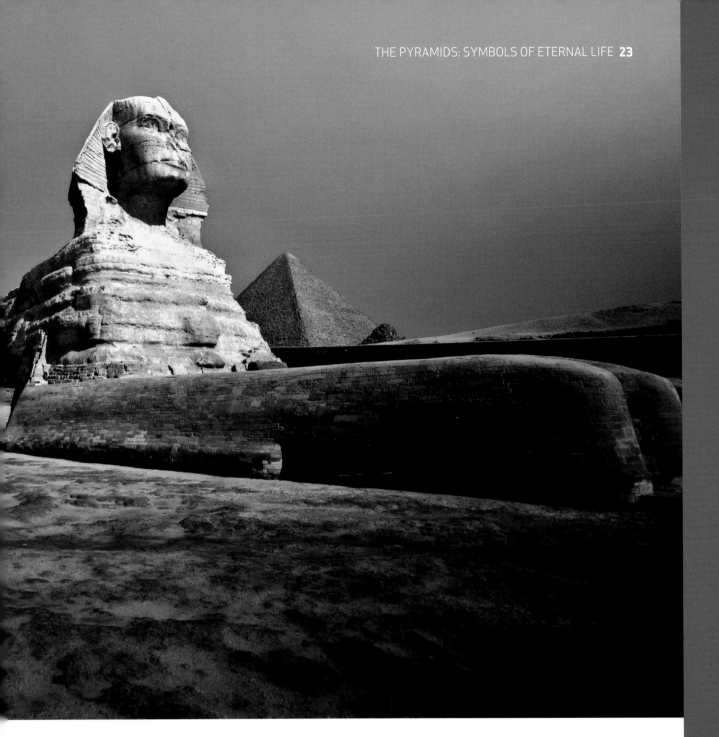

that their shape reflects the concept of the world held by the ancient inhabitants of the banks of the Nile. They considered that the universe was created from the "primeval hill," where the creator god brought order amidst chaos. And small hills are precisely what are first observed in the fields of Egypt when the water from the Nile starts to retract after the floods.

These hills of earth have been fertilized by the waters and give food and life to the people. Thus, the pyramids could be considered a stylization of that "primeval hill," and their shape the result of a progression that began with the first known pyramid, that of Zoser, a tiered construction in which stone was first used as a constructive material. Bear in mind

that in hieroglyphics, the term for pyramid is "mer," meaning "ladder." A staircase that would take the Pharaoh's soul to the abode of the gods and through which he could also descend to his kingdom on earth, perhaps to continue care for his people from the afterlife.

THE SPHINX OF GIZA
Carved from a large limestone ledge in Giza, it is believed to represent the Pharaoh Khafra, who commissioned the work, with a lion's body. It measures 65.61 ft (20 m) high and 236.22 ft long (72 m). Behind it, to the right, is the pyramid of Khufu, and to its left the pyramid of Khafra.

This tiered pyramid, built during the third dynasty of Egypt near the main necropolis of Memphis on the eastern bank of the Nile River around 30 km (18.6 mi) from Cairo and 17 km (10.5 mi) from Giza, was the prototype of the Pyramids of Giza.

A Different Necropolis

Prior to the construction of the Pyramid of Zoser in the Saqqara necropolis, the royal tombs consisted of underground chambers covered by an adobe structure in the shape of a truncated pyramid (mastaba). The Pyramid of Zoser is formed by six enormous mastabas, one on top of the other, and it is the first monument of Ancient Egypt made with carved stone.

A MILESTONE This pyramid is considered to be the world's largest stone structure and it was built by Imhotep, the first known architect in history.

How Were the Pyramids Built?

How was it possible to erect a structure thousands of years ago that remained the tallest stone structure in the world until well into the nineteenth century? What techniques did the Egyptians use? Scholars are still looking for a conclusive answer.

The first description of the methods used to build the Pyramid of Khufu is given by the Greek historian Herodotus in his Book II (*Euterpe*). "This pyramid," he wrote was built on a hill in a succession of steps that some call ledges or crossai and others stone slabs or bomides (...). The upper part of the pyramid was finished first, followed by the lower part." Herodotus' description was considered reliable until the nineteenth century when, as the interior of the pyramid was seen, unknown factors increased.

Today the majority of Egyptologists agree that the following steps were used in the construction process:

1. Leveling. Between 1880 and 1882, British Archaeologist Sir William Matthew Flinders Petrie (1853–1942) performed one of the first scientific studies on the Giza Plateau. It then emerged that Egyptians of the fourth dynasty would have stabilized and leveled the area on which they would build the Great Pyramid, digging into the rock on which a network of shallow trenches that would have been filled with water would be made. Then, they would reduce or increase the depth of the excavation until they had perfectly leveled the ground on which the great stone structure would be built. One century later, Egyptologist Mark Lehner, author of *The Complete Pyramids of Egypt* and creator of a detailed map of the Giza Plateau, argued that in reality the Egyptians would not have treated the entire area occupied by the pyramid, but they would have ensured the perfect horizontality of the support base using the water level of narrow trenches dug underneath the borders.

2. Alignment. It is evident that the ancient Egyptians used their knowledge of astronomy to draw the lines and angles of their buildings and to orient the sides and corners of their structures according to the alignment of the stars. To do so, they used instruments and tools for observing the stars such as the *merkhet* (instrument used by the Egyptians to measure time, similar to an astrolabe) – a horizontal bar carved out of bone that had a plumb line hung from a transverse hole placed at the end and that was controlled with a wooden handle – and the *bay*, made with a palm leaf rib cut in the shape of a "V." Both instruments, whose margin of error was around 0.5 degrees, could have been used in a very precise manner to locate

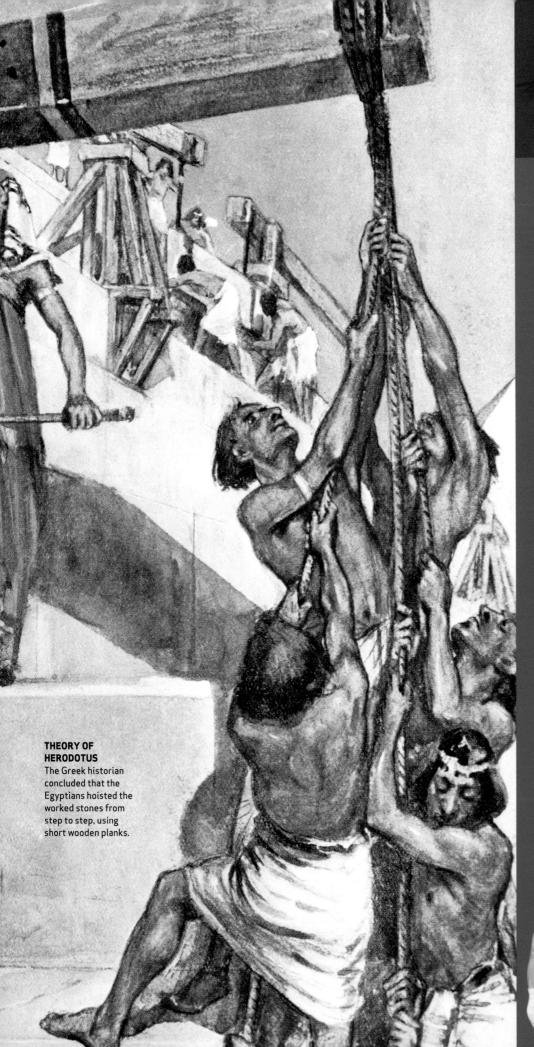

THEORY OF HERODOTUS
The Greek historian concluded that the Egyptians hoisted the worked stones from step to step, using short wooden planks.

enigmas

How Did They Shape the Stones Used to Build the Pyramids?

There are still uncertainties today about the technology that was applied for working the stones with which the pyramids were erected. Professor Michel Barsoum published an article in the *National Science Foundation* in which he puts forth that those stones were not cut or carved but were cast with an ancient technology for cement. Barsoum based this on a work by Joseph Davidovits from the Geopolymer Institute in Quintin, France, who stated that the stones of the pyramids were made up of a kind of concrete in which limestone, clay, lime, and water were mixed together. However, other researchers continue to think that the stones were carved from a natural block of limestone.

the cardinal points and they were also used in the *pedj shes* ("stretching the cord") ceremonies prior to starting construction, based on the observation of Ursa Major and the circumpolar stars.

3. Underground Chamber. Once the land was leveled and the alignment of the future pyramid established, the construction of the underground chamber, excavated in rocky subsoil, would have started. In the case of the Great Pyramid, it has a rectangular floor and two rooms, a shaft and a small underground chamber accessed by a descending passage that in reality, is an extension of the one that goes to the entrance of the pyramid. The chamber is connected to the room called the Grand Gallery by an almost vertical tunnel. The purpose of this room could have been to house a hoist for lifting stone blocks through the tunnel.

4. Ramps. Although there are no longer remnants of ramps around the Great Pyramid of Giza, the majority of Archaeologists agree that these would have been used to move the millions of stone blocks used in building the pyramids, since remnants have been found in other similar structures. It is thought that different systems were used: a smooth, inclined ramp (probably used in the Step Pyramid of Zoser, in Saqqara) or several ramps, in a step configuration or in a zigzag, that rested on each of the faces of the pyramid and connected the rows of stones. One of the latest theories in this regard is the one formulated by French architect Jean-Pierre Houdin in 2007, after a microgravity test done in 1986 on the

Great Pyramid. He detected a less dense structure in the shape of a spiral inside the building. According to this researcher, the Egyptians would have used an external ramp of around 40 m (131.2 ft), and from there would have constructed another internal spiral-shaped one with an inclination of seven degrees, and openings on the corners through which the stone blocks would have been inserted.

QUARRIES AND TOOLS

It has been calculated that 2,521,999 m³ (89,063,553.78 ft³) of stone in rectangular and square blocks, that each weighed a minimum of two tons, was used for building the Great Pyramid of Pharaoh Khufu.

The King's Chamber was originally covered with around 27,000 pieces of white polished limestone, of which there were still remnants at the beginning of the sixteenth century. It seems that the majority of these blocks were cut in quarries near the pyramid construction area, though others were transported on the Nile River in barges. There has been much discussion over the techniques that the Egyptians of the fourth dynasty used to cut and polish these blocks. It seems that they did so with saws with a copper alloy blade, together with quartz grains moistened with water, a system that delayed the wear of the metal and made use of quart's abrasive properties.

Recently, flint and diorite hammers and limestone balls that when reduced to dust could be used as mortar, were discovered on the plain around Giza.

BUILDING THE PYRAMID

The amazing Egyptians must have had advanced planning technology and a constant supply of resources to ensure that the pyramids were finished during the life of the kings. Tons of rocks, some from the site itself and others brought from several kilometers away, needed to be moved and piled up to build the monuments.

THE STONES

Each block weighs around 2.5 tons on average. Their dimensions are irregular since they get progressively smaller towards the top. The weight of two of these stones is equivalent to that of an African elephant.

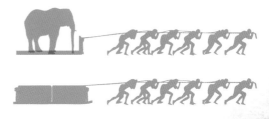

THE RAMPS

The Egyptians must have built ramps and slopes for moving the stones. These slopes were made of limestone, gravel, and plaster so that they could easily be taken apart and removed after finishing the monument.

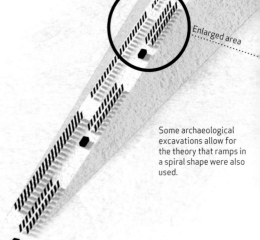

Enlarged area

Some archaeological excavations allow for the theory that ramps in a spiral shape were also used.

DEVELOPMENT

The side ramps and spiral ramps ascended as the structure was completed. They were removed when it was finished.

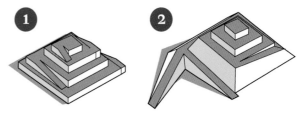

① ②

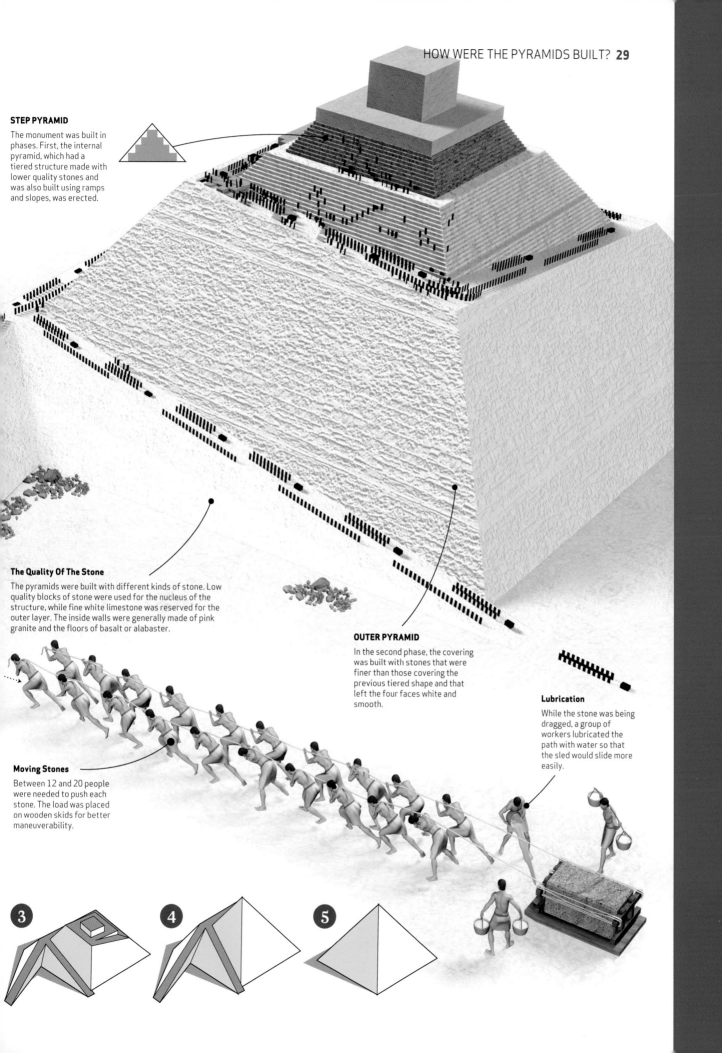

STEP PYRAMID

The monument was built in phases. First, the internal pyramid, which had a tiered structure made with lower quality stones and was also built using ramps and slopes, was erected.

The Quality Of The Stone

The pyramids were built with different kinds of stone. Low quality blocks of stone were used for the nucleus of the structure, while fine white limestone was reserved for the outer layer. The inside walls were generally made of pink granite and the floors of basalt or alabaster.

OUTER PYRAMID

In the second phase, the covering was built with stones that were finer than those covering the previous tiered shape and that left the four faces white and smooth.

Lubrication

While the stone was being dragged, a group of workers lubricated the path with water so that the sled would slide more easily.

Moving Stones

Between 12 and 20 people were needed to push each stone. The load was placed on wooden skids for better maneuverability.

Were They Built by Slaves?

Twenty years ago, a tourist's horse stumbled over a piece of a buried wall at the leveled area of Giza. It was remnants of what would later be named "The Cemetery of the Pyramid Builders." This discovery provided crucial information.

The excavation, carried out by Mark Lehner and Zahi Hawass, refuted the old theory that the pyramids had been built by slaves. The burial sites found were in the sacred and ceremonial area of the leveled area of Giza, to the south of the pyramids and the Sphinx. If they had belonged to slaves, they would not have been placed that close to the Pharaohs. Until recently, the tombs of 30 foremen and around 600 workers were known, but new burial grounds were recently discovered which confirm that the work of building the pyramids was done by free men who collaborated in a large-scale communal project in which the entire society of the time was involved. According to Hawass, the number of workers would have been around 10,000. They performed their functions for three months and were then replaced by others once this period of time ended. Those that died while building the pyramids were buried at the site, and there was health care for the sick and injured. From the human remains found, it is deduced that emergency treatments such as resetting bones were used. There is evidence of some cases of amputations and of degenerative arthritis in the lumbar area and the knees of some of the workers, likely consequences of the enormous effort required to lift large amounts of weight.

Among the most notable of recently discovered tombs is a rectangular one with an outer covering of plastered bricks that has several shafts and funeral niches and belonged to an individual named Idu. The tomb's outer part has a domed shape, which is a symbol of the first hill where the ancient Egyptians believed creation started. This tells experts that it was built during the fourth dynasty, at the same time that the Great Pyramid was built.

Currently, it is estimated that only 5 % of the total area of this large workers' cemetery has been excavated. In some of the tombs, the office of the worker that was buried there is written. Titles such as "supervisor of builders," "head of artisans" or "head of workers' bakery" have been found, which confirm the existence of a complex and detailed work organization.

The Workers' Village

The necropolis discovered to the southeast of the Pyramid of Menkaure is proof that there must have been a major city nearby in which the daily lives of those who built the pyramids was carried out. A city (in the photo) has been found, which Mark Lehner continues excavating, which includes a storage and production center, three paved streets, and other large structures. The pyramid project permitted the workers to prosper in the best of cases, and in the worst to be buried close to the mausoleums of the kings. To the ancient Egyptians, this meant there was a chance that the pharaoh would intercede for the salvation of their souls and was nearly a guarantee of access to the afterlife.

Very Well-Fed Workers

On the outskirts of the "Cemetery of the Pyramid Builders" in Giza, remains were found that confirm that the pyramid workers were very well nourished. Recently, a large number of cow and fish bones (in the image, a bas-relief from the time shows two men fishing in the Nile River), enough to feed thousands of men for several years, were discovered. The supervisors of the Giza excavations calculated and estimated that the families of Egypt donated 21 head of cattle and 23 sheep every day to feed the workers who built the pyramids. The beef and fish were generally grilled or dried and preserved in salt. The most valued fish was the mullet, a saltwater fish that lives in the Nile River.

Construction Work

The massive effort required to build the Egyptian pyramids is an unmistakable reflection of the wealth and the central power held by Pharaohs from the Old Kingdom such as Zoser, Snefru, Khufu, and Khafra, as well as the organizational capacity of this society to carry out the task.

THE WORKFORCE

According to the information provided by experts such as Craig B. Smith, author of *How the Great Pyramid Was Built*, and the famous Egyptologist Zahi Hawass, 4,000 stone cutters, in addition to quarry workers, stone transporters, carpenters, smelters, brick makers, and tool sharpeners worked on the Great Pyramid of Khufu.

ORGANIZATIONAL CAPACITY

The Egyptians must have had planning and management methods for managing tasks, and the efficacy of these tools is even more striking when the precarious means they had to work with are taken into account.

The Ramps

Each ramp used during the construction process could have been the size of two thirds the volume of the pyramids. It is thought that they were made of adobe brick compartments filled with sand.

WEIGHT OF THE BLOCKS
It is estimated that the stone blocks each weighed between 2 and 15 tons (1.8 to 13.6 metric tons).

Why Are They Aligned with the Stars?

The ancient Egyptians knew about the North Star, Sirius, and constellations such as Ursa Major. It is believed that they used this knowledge to precisely align the pyramids with certain stars.

Herodotus was correct in stating that the Egyptians were the most religious of all people, since everything in life in that culture was permeated by the presence of the divine element.

However, the Egyptian religion was not based on accepting dogma but on practicing worship, and the most ancient worship had to do with the cosmic gods that are embodied in the forms of nature.

It is clear that since the most ancient times the Egyptians made observing the sky an essential practice, and they became very precise in their observations. For them, for example, the 12 hours of the night had equivalents in 12 stars they associated with the "12 Guardians of the Sky," whose mission was to accompany the dead Pharaohs in their nighttime journey through the sky in the boat of Ra, the Sun God. Therefore, it was of vital importance that the pyramids be well oriented with the stars, since they were the stopover of the Pharaohs on their way to a life after death. Robert Bauval (Alexandria, 1948) and Graham Hancock (Edinburgh, 1950) stated in their book *The Orion Mystery: Unlocking the Secrets of the Pyramids*, published in 1990, that the pyramids of Giza represent the likeness of Orion's belt on the earth's surface. Scientists do not give credit to this speculation, since this constellation is of Mesopotamian origin and would not have been known in Egypt for a long time after the pyramids were built.

More recently, Kate Spence, Egyptologist from the University of Cambridge, presented a theory regarding the orientation of the Great Pyramid: the Egyptian architects could have aligned the building with two circumpolar stars that rotate around true North: Kochab (b Ursa Minor) and Mizar (z Ursa Major) which could have been perfectly aligned around the year 2467 BCE and which would provide the exact date on which the Great Pyramid could have been built.

The Hypotheses is reinforced because the inaccuracies in the orientations of the previous and subsequent pyramids seem to correspond with the degrees of deviation from North of these two stars at different times.

The Star Belt

This is the speculation formulated by Robert Bauval and Graham Hancock in their book *The Orion Mystery: Unlocking the Secrets of the Pyramids*.
In the book they claimed that the pyramids of Giza represent the likeness of Orion's Belt (the stars Alnilam, Mintaka and Alnitak) on the earth's surface, based on the

knowledge of Egyptian astronomy applied to the design and location of these structures. According to this Hypotheses, the pyramids would be tombs oriented towards the stars for the purpose of facilitating the passing of the Pharaohs to the afterlife in accordance with the religious beliefs of Ancient Egypt.

ALNILAM   MINTAKA

ALNITAK

enigmas

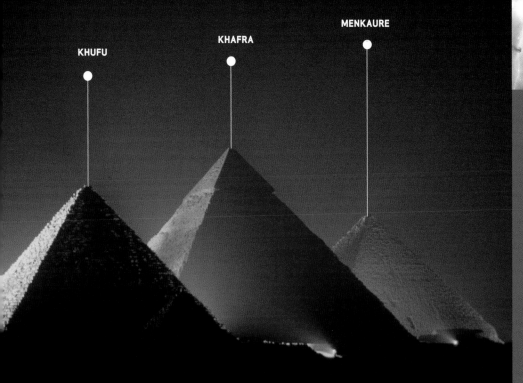

KHUFU   KHAFRA   MENKAURE

The Constellation of Orion, a Point of Reference for the Egyptians

Currently, the three stars of Orion form an angle that differs by a few degrees from the angle along which the pyramids were built. However, if the precessional changes of Orion's Belt are calculated over the centuries, it is confirmed that there was a time when these three stars were in the exact same alignment with the Milky Way as the pyramids are with the Nile River: around 10,500 BCE. The expert Robert Bauval made these calculations for his book *The Orion Mystery* and speculates that the master project of the pyramids of Giza was conceived during this time. It is thought that the Pyramids of Dahshur, Abusir, Zawyet el-Aryan and Abu Rawash also have their likenesses in the sky.

Isis

The Egyptian triangle is rectangular and its sides have a length of 3, 4, and 5 (or its measurements keep these proportions). In Ancient Egypt, with the measurements of 15, 20, and 25 cubits, it was called the "Isis" triangle—after the goddess Isis, whose Egyptian name was Ast—and was used to obtain right angles in the architectural structures. Its area is 6 (the first perfect number) and the cube of its area is equal to the sum of the cubes of its sides.

SACRED GEOMETRY
The knowledge of geometry, considered sacred, was kept secret to the priests. It came from Babylon and influenced Ancient Egypt.

CRITERIA
Experts claim that the builders of the Great Pyramid tried to square the circle.

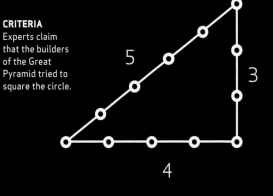

5

3

4

What Was Hidden Inside Them?

Generally, there were no rooms or passageways inside the pyramids. The "subterranean chambers," as they are known, were excavated in the rock, beneath the first level of stones. The pyramids of Meidum and Khufu are the exception.

The pyramids' burial chambers were usually found below the pyramids. They were reached by a passage descending from the north side, where the Pharaoh's spirit would exit toward the circumpolar stars that were identified with the king himself. The King's Chamber lies inside the pyramid's structure in only two of these buildings: the pyramid of Meidum, completed during the time of the Pharaoh Snefru, father of Khufu – which was originally a step pyramid that was later finished with smooth walls – and the Great Pyramid. Thus, the structures and passages hidden in the interior of Khufu's pyramid, even today, continue to generate mystery. Meanwhile, the fact remains: no Pharaoh's mummy has ever been found inside a pyramid.

COMPLEX STRUCTURE

The structure of the Great Pyramid has five main elements:
1) The Subterranean Chamber; 2) the Queen's Chamber—in which no queen was ever buried, but which was so named by the Arabs because of its gabled roof, which they identified with feminine sepulchers; 3) the Grand Gallery, an ascending passage nearly 47 m (154.2 ft) long and 8 m (26.3 ft) high, considered a master architectural work, with smooth walls up to 2 m (6.6 ft) high, after which the rows of stone begin to move closer toward each other to form a vault; 4) the Antechamber, through which the King's Chamber is reached; and 5) the King's Chamber, in which only a granite sarcophagus was found. This must have been placed there during the construction of the pyramid, seeing as it is much wider than the access passages. The ceiling in this chamber is made of nine stone slabs with relieving chambers. The last of these is vaulted, in order to distribute the immense pressure of the blocks from the pyramid, so that the entire weight does not fall on the Royal Chamber.

In addition to the rooms, there are several access corridors – descending, horizontal and ascending – as well as the so-called "air shafts," which seem to connect the burial chambers of the King and Queen with the exterior (from the center of the structure). However, their real function remains unknown.

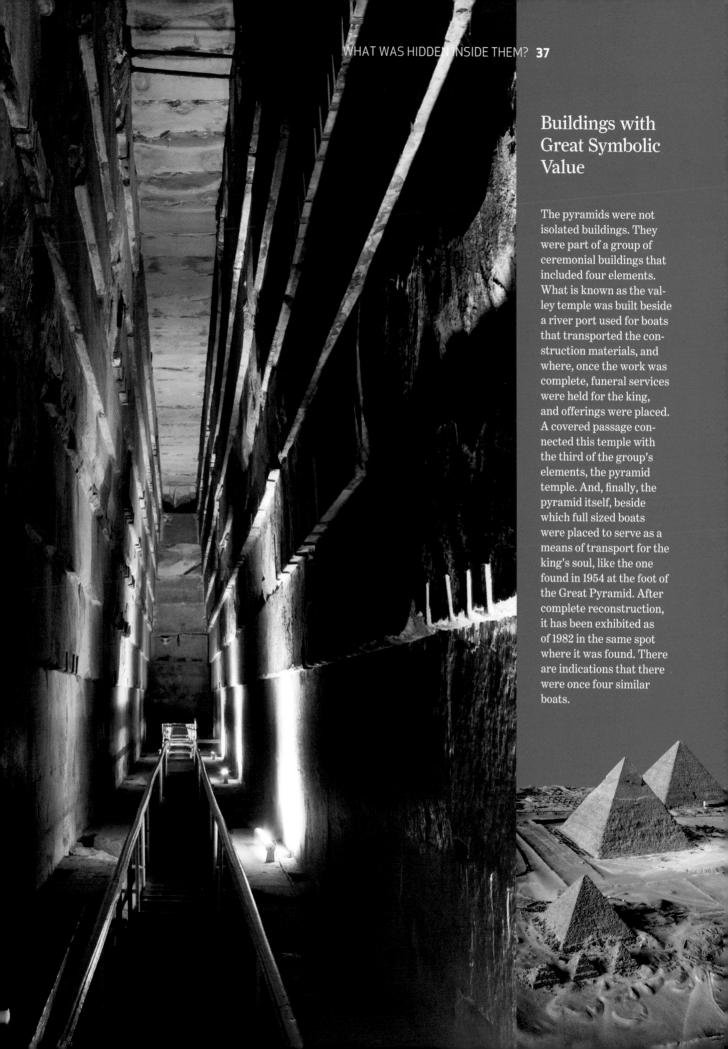

Buildings with Great Symbolic Value

The pyramids were not isolated buildings. They were part of a group of ceremonial buildings that included four elements. What is known as the valley temple was built beside a river port used for boats that transported the construction materials, and where, once the work was complete, funeral services were held for the king, and offerings were placed. A covered passage connected this temple with the third of the group's elements, the pyramid temple. And, finally, the pyramid itself, beside which full sized boats were placed to serve as a means of transport for the king's soul, like the one found in 1954 at the foot of the Great Pyramid. After complete reconstruction, it has been exhibited as of 1982 in the same spot where it was found. There are indications that there were once four similar boats.

Robot Explorers

The pyramid of Khufu has four narrow shafts whose function remains a mystery. Two of them begin in the King's Chamber and lead to the outside; the other two begin in the Queen's Chamber, and it is not known where they end. Small robots with cameras have been built to explore them.

The Mission's Objective

What is the purpose of the shafts in Khufu's pyramid? Researchers hired by the Egyptian government tried to answer this question, but they only thing they could determine with certainty is how they were built.

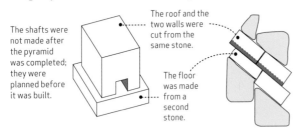

The shafts were not made after the pyramid was completed; they were planned before it was built.

The roof and the two walls were cut from the same stone.

The floor was made from a second stone.

The Upuaut Robots

The first robot explorer built was the Upuaut ("the opener of the ways"). A short time later an improved version, the Upuaut-2, was completed (drawing).

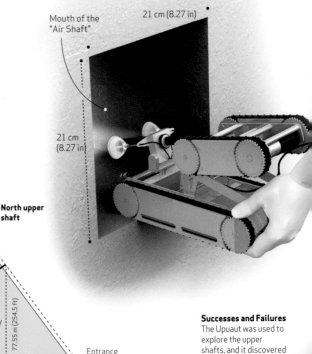

Mouth of the "Air Shaft"

21 cm (8.27 in)

21 cm (8.27 in)

Successes and Failures
The Upuaut was used to explore the upper shafts, and it discovered that they opened to the outside. The Upuaut-2 was sent to traverse the lower shafts, but obstacles were found preventing its passage.

The Shafts

The two upper shafts have been known since the seventeenth century. The two lower ones were discovered by British engineer Waynman Dixon in 1872.

South upper shaft

North upper shaft

King's Chamber

78.43 m (257.3 ft)

77.55 m (254.5 ft)

Grand Gallery

Entrance

Original outline of pyramid.

South lower shaft

Queen's Chamber

North lower shaft

0 10 20 meters

South ←→ North

Subterranean Chamber

Exploration with Robots

In 1933, the Egyptian government decided to install an air conditioning system in the Great Pyramid – in order to protect it from the humidity caused by tourist visits – using the improperly named "air shafts." The task was assigned to German engineer Rudolf Gantenbrink, who designed the Upuaut robot, and later the Upuaut-2.

1 **1993**
Gantenbrink sent a robot into the south lower shaft and discovered a slab blocking the shaft. It was named Gantenbrink's Door.

2 **2002**
A new expedition sent in another robot with a drill and a fiberoptic camera, which showed another slab behind Gantenbrink's Door.

3 **2002**
Not much later, a robot was sent through the north lower shaft, and another door similar and equidistant to Gantenbrink's was discovered.

The Only Objects

Only three objects have been found inside the pyramid of Khufu. Waynman Dixon found them in 1872, when he discovered the shafts from the Queen's Chamber. They include an anchor-like double hook (photo), a granite ball, and a cedar rod, all placed at the entrance to the lower north-facing shaft.

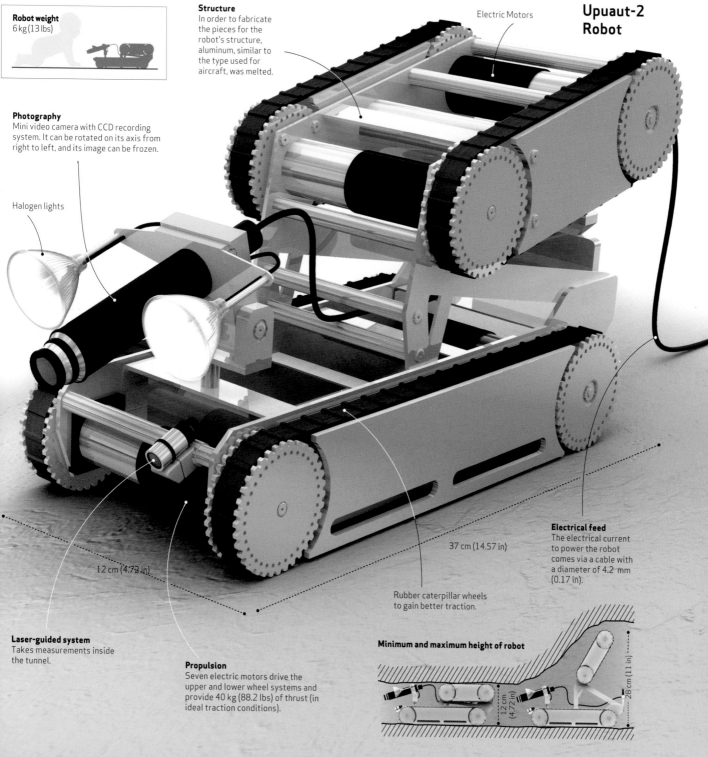

Robot weight
6 kg (13 lbs)

Structure
In order to fabricate the pieces for the robot's structure, aluminum, similar to the type used for aircraft, was melted.

Electric Motors

Upuaut-2 Robot

Photography
Mini video camera with CCD recording system. It can be rotated on its axis from right to left, and its image can be frozen.

Halogen lights

12 cm (4.73 in)

37 cm (14.57 in)

Electrical feed
The electrical current to power the robot comes via a cable with a diameter of 4.2 mm (0.17 in).

Rubber caterpillar wheels to gain better traction.

Laser-guided system
Takes measurements inside the tunnel.

Propulsion
Seven electric motors drive the upper and lower wheel systems and provide 40 kg (88.2 lbs) of thrust (in ideal traction conditions).

Minimum and maximum height of robot

12 cm (4.72 in)

28 cm (11 in)

What Do the Pyramid Texts Reveal?

The Pyramid Texts are the most ancient and complete collection of religious writings in the world: prayers, petitions, spells, magical formulas and invocations, the ultimate meaning of which is not yet fully known.

In 1880, the excavators working in the Saqqara plains, some 15 km (9.3 mi) southwest of Cairo, entered the pyramid of Pepi I, the third Pharaoh of the sixth dynasty. Some months later, they discovered the pyramid of Unas, the last pharaoh of the fifth dynasty. They worked under the direction of French Archaeologist Gaston Maspero (1846–1916), who is considered the discoverer of the Pyramid Texts. It is not difficult to imagine his surprise at finding that the antechamber and burial chamber of the Pharaoh Unas were almost completely covered with long columns of funeral rites inscribed in blue-green tinted bas-relief. The ceilings had also been decorated, with yellow stars on a blue background. Only the west wall of the Pharaoh's chamber was empty of inscriptions. These were the first texts that had been found in a pyramid, and to this day are the most ancient to have been found. They include 228 sentences that appear to have been written for the purpose of helping the Pharaoh in his journey to the afterlife.

COMPLEX INTERPRETATION

The Pyramid Texts were also pivotal for science, as they helped provide an understanding of the history of religion in Ancient Egypt, although their translation and interpretation were very difficult. Maspero himself was the first to try, and to this day, while 759 statements are known (compiled in 1969 by R. Faulkner), translations and grammar have proliferated, and knowledge of the Egyptian language has become a genuine discipline, controversy remains. After that discovery, more texts were discovered in the pyramids of Pharaohs Pepi I and II, of the sixth dynasty; in those of queens Nedjeftet, Udjebten and Iput; and that of Pharaoh Qakare Ibi, from the eighth dynasty. It was then revealed that some passages also appeared to be engraved into the tombs and sarcophagi of the kings of the Middle Kingdom, in papyri in the New Kingdom, and in what is called the Late Period. With the passage of time, these texts became the basis for what is known as the *Book of the Dead*, which describes what the spirit of the deceased must do to achieve immortality. Its contents would undergo later evolution through to the twenty-sixth dynasty, when not only the Pharaohs had the possibility of access to the afterlife, but immortality was also within reach of "ordinary Egyptians" – that is, those who could pay for their bodies to be embalmed and for the rituals required to reach eternal life.

Types of Writing

In Ancient Egypt, hieroglyphic, hieratic (also called cursive) and demotic writing were used. The first dates from the end of the Early Dynastic period (3100 BCE), hieratic from the Old Kingdom (2700 BCE), and demotic was used beginning in the eighth century BCE. In hieroglyphics, ideograms were mixed with another type of sign. The symbols, some 700, were generally figurative. Scholars still do not agree entirely on the reading order and correspondence of specific sounds and meanings. Hieratic writing was simpler, and was reserved for religious and priestly texts and written on papyrus and ceramic or wood tablets. As of the twenty-sixth dynasty, it was replaced by demotic writing, a simplification of hieratic writing, used in regular everyday documents.

Egyptian Hieroglyphics

The writing system used in Ancient Egypt from 3100 BCE through 400 CE could not be deciphered until the nineteenth century. The finding of the Rosetta Stone allowed the true meaning of a complex symbology to be discovered.

The Rosetta Stone

A black granite stone on which three different forms of writing were inscribed: hieroglyphic, demotic, and Greek. It was discovered on July 15 1799 by soldiers of Napoleon's army near the city of el-Rashid (Rosetta). It contains a decree from Pharaoh Ptolemy V.

Starting from the Greek inscriptions, scientists were able to begin to decipher the hieroglyphics.

Thomas Young (United Kingdom)
Was the first to show that the hieroglyphics on the Rosetta Stone corresponded to the sounds of a real name, that of Ptolemy.

Jean-François Champollion (France)
Confirmed that the hieroglyphics reproduced the sounds of the Egyptian language and established the basis of understanding of the language and culture of Ancient Egypt.

The text found on the stone is a decree issued by a council of priests that ratified the royal cult of Ptolemy V, 13 years of age, on the first anniversary of his coronation.

Hieroglyphic Text (writing of the gods)

.... Enlarged text ....

Hieroglyphics were not written in linear sequence, one after the other, like the letters of an alphabetic system, but rather were grouped in imaginary squares or rectangles, to ensure the most harmonious arrangement and to minimize the possibility of ugly empty spaces.

114 cm (44.9 in)

Demotic text (writing of the people)

Uncial Greek Text (writing of the government)

72 cm (28.3 in)   27 cm (10.6 in)

The Hieroglyphic Writing System

The Egyptian hieroglyphic writing system is mixed: ideographic and consonantal. Thus, it is made up of:

IDEOGRAMS
Signs that represent objects exclusively in graphic form.

PHONOGRAMS
Signs that represent the pronunciation of a letter.

SYLLABIC
Signs that represent the pronunciation of more than one consonant.

DETERMINATIVES
Signs that act as markers in words to indicate their semantic function.

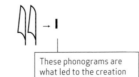 → **r'** → Ra = Day / Sun

 → **I**

These phonograms are what led to the creation of an alphabet.

→ **nb** → neb

→ **iwn** → iun

→ **rnpt** → renepet

 → Forward

→ Back

The hieroglyphic alphabet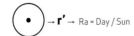

| a | a | b | c / k | ch | d | e | f | g | h | h | i | kh (j) | kh (j) |

The Tomb of Pepi I

Pepi I was the third Pharaoh of the sixth dynasty of Egypt, and governed from c. 2310 to 2260 BCE. His pyramid is found in South Saqqara, and the famous Pyramid Texts, analyzed by so many scholars, were engraved in his chamber. This hieroglyph, found in Saqqara (photo) means, according to specialists, "Pepi, son of Ra." To the Egyptians, Ra was one of the names of the Sun. During the day, Ra illuminated the Earth in the form of a falcon.

READING DIRECTION

The Egyptians wrote both left to right and right to left. Thomas Young was the first to discover that the reading direction of the hieroglyphics was determined by the orientation of the heads of figures such as animals.

The names of the Pharaohs or queens were enclosed in cartouches.

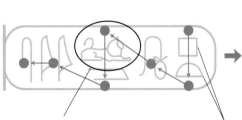

The heads face the beginning of words and indicate reading direction.

The upper has priority over the lower.

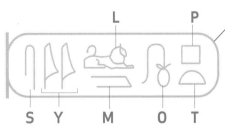

With the help of the Rosetta Stone, sounds were assigned to the symbols.

→ **PTOLEMYS**
(Ptolemy)

| j | l | m | m | n | o | p | q | r | s/z | s | t | u(w) | w | y | y |

Alternative Hypotheses

Were the Pyramids Designed by the Atlanteans?

To those who believe in the existence of Atlantis, the pyramids of Giza are considered tangible proof of the influence that this supposedly superior and lost culture had on the major civilizations of antiquity. According to Edgar Cayce, one of the most famous American clairvoyants, the great pyramid was built through a combined effort of the Egyptians – who provided the manual labor, and the architects of Atlantis – who contributed their knowledge and their particular genius to the construction.

Cayce believed there was a political and social objective to this effort: to assimilate immigrants from the west – the Atlanteans – into the indigenous population through a common project. Kurt Mendelssohn, Oxford University Professor, arrived at the same conclusion in 1971, but not related to the Atlanteans; he considered the construction of the pyramids a way to occupy farmers during periods of inactivity between farming seasons. As Mendelssohn saw it, these buildings were social welfare programs, and not the work of slaves, but rather large groups of workers who received their daily pay in food.

EDGAR CAYCE
The American clairvoyant states that he has found signs of Atlantis in Egypt.

Did the Pyramids Have Energizing Effects?

In 1859 the scientist Werner von Siemens, creator of the famous German company Siemens, climbed to the top of the pyramid of Khufu and, raising his arms to the sky, noted a strong tingling sensation throughout his body, which led him to conclude that the pyramids attracted static electricity. But what effect did that have? So arose a question to which the answer would, apparently, be revealed in 1930 by the French technician and radiesthesist Antoine Bovis, who traveled to Egypt with his pendulum to take measurements. Bovis observed dead animals in the passages and chambers of the Great Pyramid that had been naturally mummified. According to the radiesthesist, the pyramid acted as a preservative device whose greatest preservative power pointed directly to the King's Chamber, where it is assumed that the body of the Pharaoh, which was never found, had been. Later, the parapsychologist Max Toth put forth that the pyramids helped maintain a positive energy level in individuals and even improved their spirituality.

Is the Great Pyramid an Astronomical Table?

Obsession over the dimensions of the Great Pyramid and its astronomical, geographic, divine, and prophetic repercussions has been unceasing since the middle of the nineteenth century. In 1859, John Taylor published his book *The Great Pyramid: Why Was It Built? And Who Built It?*, in which the English writer used the measurements made by French engineers during Napoleon's expedition to Egypt and deduced that the Egyptians had used a unit of measure one thousand times greater than one modern British inch. Making calculations based on this unit of measure, he began to see surprising results: for example, that the total length of the four sides of the pyramid was 36,524 pyramidal inches (one hundred times the number of days in a year). Some time later, the Scottish astronomer Charles Piazzi Smyth traveled to Egypt and took new measurements of the pyramid of Khufu. The incidences of terrestrial measurements and those of the solar system coinciding were multiplied to the point that these experts

confidently proclaimed that the pyramidal inch must have derived from some superior and perhaps divine being. It was even proposed that the height of a pyramid could be converted into years and predict the end of the world, or provide the exact date of the birth of Jesus Christ.
In the twentieth century, Egyptologists soon refuted these calculations – both the measurements and their astronomical and geographical comparisons – since the prophetic repercussions had been addressed earlier. In any case, some modern Egyptologists maintain that the large amount of Biblical and astronomical links invented by Piazzi Smyth ended up unintentionally covering up relationships that do exist between some dimensions of the Great Pyramid of the Pharaoh Khufu and the measurements of the Earth. It would come to be confirmed that the monument always had a direct and proportional relationship with certain geographical and astronomical knowledge that the Egyptians had possessed in those distant times.

METHODOLOGY According to two Argentine scholars, nearly all of the pharaonic monuments in Egypt were carved from bare rock.

Were the Pyramids Carved from the Top Down?

According to Argentine professors Edmundo Ashkar and Amalia Frontini, the pyramids were not built from the ground up, but rather from the top down, carved out of an existing limestone rock formation and following the shadow projected by the previous step on the rock. They point out the lack of evidence of ramps, and put forth that if the pyramids had been built by placing one block of rock on top of the other, such blocks would also be seen from inside.

Alternative Hypotheses

Where Is the Mummy of Pharaoh Khufu?

The official theory states that the tomb of Khufu was raided at the beginning of the reign of Menkaure, his grandson. Khufu had carried out a religious revolution in order to unite the power of the State fully under his command. But his grandson – with the support of the priests – intended to erase all signs of these reforms, and may have ordered the destruction of his tomb. However, other hypotheses put forth that, foreseeing the pillaging he would suffer after his death, Khufu's faithful buried the Pharaoh's body in a hidden location in the Great Pyramid. Herodotus speaks of this possibility, writing that the body of the Pharaoh rests in a crypt excavated in the rock, at the level of the waters at the bottom of the Nile. In 2004, Gilles Dormion, architect and Egyptian scholar, proposed in his book *The Chamber of Cheops* the existence of a fourth secret space under the Queen's Chamber, where Khufu's sarcophagus would rest. To date, the Egyptian Supreme Council of Antiquities (SCA) has refused authorization to explore the pyramid. The refusal is on the grounds that, among other things, Dormion had acted on a similar hunch to conduct an excavation in 1986 and found nothing but sand.

The search for the Pharaoh's body continues to this day, although most Egyptologists assume it was destroyed in one of the innumerable Egyptian, Christian, or Muslim religious revolts, or that it may have disappeared during the hunt for mummies that began in the Middle Ages.

ASHES OF KHUFU
In the seventeenth century, cylindrical receptacles like those in this image began to circulate, which supposedly contained the ashes of Khufu and other Pharaohs. It was said the ashes had aphrodisiac powers.

Is the Pyramid of Menkaure the Tomb of a Courtesan?

The first to speak of this possibility was Herodotus (430 BCE), who, in his work, does not deny the story because it is absurd, but rather because he believes a courtesan could not have had enough money to pay for such a work to be built. Several centuries later, the historian Diodorus Siculus (56 BCE) repeats the story, and asserts that provincial governors, who were her lovers, paid for the construction of the pyramid. The famous geographer and historian Strabo (64 BCE–19 BCE) gives the Hypotheses that Rhodopis, the name of the courtesan in question, could have paid for a pyramid by means of her profession. This Hypotheses could not have impressed the more puritan-minded, since the construction of the pyramids has always been connected with brothels. Herodotus asserted that the Pharaoh Khufu, lacking the money to continue construction of his majestic pyramid, did not hesitate to use his own daughter as a prostitute to raise money and thus continue the monumental work that had been delayed.

Was There an Initial Plan for the Great Pyramid?

The Arab historian Al-Masudi cites an interview conducted by Ahmed, son of the Egyptian governor Ahmad Ibn Tulun, with an old Coptic in the year 260 of the Hegira (874 CE). According to the man interviewed, the construction of the pyramid began when the Pharaoh died. His body was placed in a large stone box and construction immediately began on the pyramid until its height was about half of the complete construction. The stone box was deposited and the work continued. However, according to the famous Egyptologist Karl Richard Lepsius (1810–1884), pyramid construction began as soon as the pharaoh took the throne, and the work advanced in stages. But the controversy persists regarding the existence of an initial plan that would be followed throughout the work. Some think that the work was modified as it was built. According to the British Egyptologist Sir W. M. Flinders Petrie (1853–1942), there would have been a complete projection when the work began, but according to the German Ludwig Borchardt (1863–1928), notable modifications were made during the course of work on the three pyramids of Giza.

Were the Pyramids Made to Withstand a Flood?

We know that the Great Pyramid was coated with white limestone from Tura, and perhaps covered with hieroglyphics. These writings could not be translated, since the plates were removed during the Middle Ages by order of Qaraqush, a Greek eunuch who was administrator for Saladin. In addition to the impressive spectacle of the pyramid with its original coating gleaming in the sun, the most significant thing for the Egyptologist would have been to understand the information recorded on those plates, if there were hieroglyphics. According to the Arab historian Al-Maqrizi (1363–1442), Pharaoh Khufu ordered the construction of the pyramid after having dreamed of a flood that would cover the earth. While the pyramid would not float like Noah's Ark, neither could it be destroyed by water or waves. Khufu ordered that numerous talismans be placed on all sides, as well as some statues of himself and his ancestors. Finally, according to some, the flood covered the Earth and covered the Great Pyramid up to the middle; according to others, it never happened. According to Maqrizi, the hieroglyphics on the white limestone plates could have provided valuable information on the matter.

PANELS WITH HIEROGLYPHICS
The historian Maqrizi believed that Khufu had the pyramid built as a refuge from a flood and that this was written in hieroglyphics.

To See and Visit

▼ **OTHER PLACES OF INTEREST**

THE MUSEM OF EGYPTIAN ANTIQUITIES
CAIRO, EGYPT

Inaugurated in 1902, the museum is a two story building located in the center of the city and surrounded by a garden decorated with antique sculptures. The ground floor, entirely dedicated to sculpture and painted reliefs, is dominated by colossal statues of Amenhotep III and Queen Tiye. The funeral furnishings of Tutankhamen are displayed on the first floor: the golden mask and sarcophagus, the jewels, and the gold throne. The collections displayed are so extensive they cannot be seen in a single day.

ALEXANDRIA NATIONAL MUSEUM
ALEXANDRIA, EGYPT

Holds collections of exotic objects from different eras of Ancient Egypt, in addition to mummies, sarcophagi, and tapestries. It is located in a restored Italian-style palace, near the center of the city. It contains approximately 1,800 archaeological objects, which contribute to a more detailed depiction of the history of Alexandria and all of Egypt. Many pieces come from other museums in the country. It was inaugurated in 2003 at the initiative of Suzanne Mubarak, the wife of (then) Egyptian president Hosni Mubarak.

BRITISH MUSEUM
LONDON, UNITED KINGDOM

The museum's Ancient Egypt section is the second most important in the world, after the Egyptian Museum in Cairo. The items displayed include jewels, papyri, paintings, and sculptures. The frequent British archaeological

The Three Pyramids of Giza

PYRAMID OF KHUFU
The three most famous Egyptian pyramids were built in the necropolis of Giza, outside of Cairo, those of Khufu (photo), Khafra, and Menkaure. The first is the largest (137 m, 449.5 ft), and served as a tomb for the Pharaoh Khufu. It is the only one of the Seven Ancient Wonders of the World that still exists. While inside it, one can see the Solar Barge of Khufu, a large boat built for ritual purposes and discovered in 1954.

PYRAMID OF KHAFRA
The construction of the second pyramid was ordered by the Pharaoh Khafra, son of Khufu. It is the only one of the three that retains its original height (which is now almost the same as that of Khufu), 136 m (446.2 ft). The best preserved part is its stone core, and little remains of the original covering. It was built on the center of a hill. The Great Sphinx, which was also built by Khafra and has the face of the Pharaoh himself, with the body of a lion, is also found in the necropolis of Giza.

PYRAMID OF MENKAURE
The smallest of the three pyramids of the necropolis on the plain of Giza, it is also known as "the Divine Pyramid." It was part of the funeral complex and had another three subsidiary pyramids, a funerary temple, the valley temple, and a processional route that connected both temples. Its interior structure is unusual: the first sixteen layers of stone are coated with red granite (most with little polish), and the rest with limestone from Tura.

Aswan, the Great Quarry

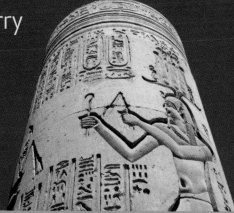

On the banks of the Nile, in the area that today covers Aswan – a city of nearly 250 thousand inhabitants located in the south of Egypt – were the stone quarries of ancient Egypt. From here, material was found to build the colossal statues, the obelisks, and, naturally, the pyramids. Under the city, there is a necropolis where the remains of the laborers who worked on the construction of the pyramids 3,000 years ago are found. Tourists also frequently visit its two monumental dams.

campaigns in Egypt are mainly due to the fact that the African country has been, since the construction of the Suez Canal (1859–69), linked to the British Empire.

IMHOTEP MUSEUM
SAQQARA, EGYPT
Dedicated to the work of the most famous architect from the time of the pharaohs, this museum is the fruit of a project directed by French archaeologist Jean-Philippe Lauer. It has five grand rooms and a significant collection of the archaeological remains found in Saqqara, where the famous stepped pyramid is found. These include the Greco-Roman period mummy found in the pyramid of Teti, and the statues of Amenhotep and his wives discovered in the pyramid complex of Unas.

STUDIUM BIBLICUM FRANCISCANUM
JERUSALEM, ISRAEL
This archaeological museum has a permanent Egyptian collection, with items ranging from the Old Kingdom through the Coptic period, including funeral objects, sculptures, and papyri.

MUSEO CIVICO ARCHEOLOGICO
BOLOGNA, ITALY
The city of Bologna houses another of the most notable Egyptian collections on the Old Continent, with more than 3,500 pieces. For those who cannot visit the museum, the web site (www.comune.bologna.it/museoarcheologico/) offers visitors a virtual reconstruction of the tomb of Horemheb in Memphis.

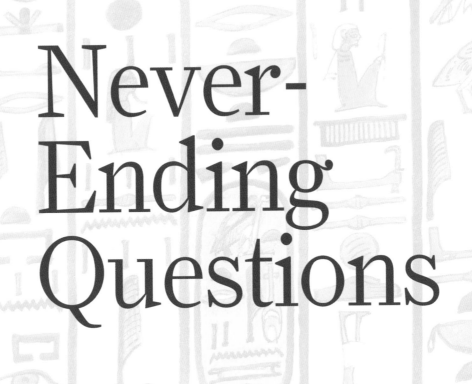

Never-Ending Questions

Egypt is a land of many mysteries, and the tales of the treasures and secrets of the pharaohs have fascinated people since the time of the ancient Greeks. A forgotten language, great antiquity, monumental ruins, buried treasure, cryptic beliefs, and magnificent gold and jewels, all make for a compelling subject. For centuries people have pondered the riddles of the sphinx and sands of Egypt, but over time, our interest and questions have only increased. This volume seeks to tackle some of the most intriguing aspects of ancient Egypt and tries to solve some of the many enigmas that surround this

remote civilization. Archaeology and genetics have combined to give us a clearer picture of who the ancient Egyptians were and where they came from. What were the reasons that people first settled the land, and how were they able to create such a long lasting and successful civilization in the middle of a barren desert? Modern science is helping to dispel the prejudices and wild speculation concerning the ancestry of the Nile Valley population.

The fate of the "heretic" Pharaoh Akhenaten and his beautiful wife Nefertiti has long intrigued people, and new theories and evidence have radically changed our ideas of the aftermath of the Amarna Age and what happened to the members of the royal family. What were the reasons that Amenhotep IV changed his name to Akhenaten? Why did he change the traditional worship of many gods to a single deity, the Aten? Did the bizarre art style he advocated reflect some sort of physical problem of the king, or were there other reasons for this strange new aesthetic?

DNA analysis recently undertaken on the royal mummies in the Cairo Museum has revealed new evidence as to what were the maladies of the most famous Egyptian dynasty and how they were related both to each other, and to the last ruler of the line, Tutankhamun. Also, we now know much more about the "boy king" and what his life was like and possibly even as to why he died so young.

The Great Sphinx of Giza is one of the world's largest and most famous sculptures, yet most do not know of its origin or purpose, and there has been much speculation as a result. How was such a massive monument created? What was its purpose? Why is it beside the most famous pyramids? Who or what does the shattered face portray? New, archaeological investigations and geological analysis have given us a much clearer picture of its construction, date and function.

The intrigue in the royal courts was no less hard to read than the smile of the Sphinx. Incest, murder and plots abounded through many of the 30 dynasties that made up the three thousand year plus history of pharaonic Egypt. New finds have shown us some more of the background to the assassination conspiracies that were hatched in the royal harems and the tangled relationships of the kings, queens, princes and princesses.

No ruling family was as troubled as Egypt's last, the Ptolemys, and their final representative, the infamous Cleopatra VII. Descended from Alexander the Great's trusted general, Ptolemy, Egypt's last dynasty were Greeks ruling Egypt in a world soon to be overshadowed by Rome. They were scientists, musicians, sybarites and scholars. Most of all, they were a family of shrewd and independent women, and none more so than the last Cleopatra. A seductress, a pawn, a genius, a statesman, a murderess, what was she really like and what was her ultimate end? All these questions surround Egypt's most famous queen, along with where is she buried?

These are just some of the many captivating mysteries that new scientific research is helping us answer. The combined work of dedicated archaeologists in the field, scientists in the laboratory and historians in dusty archives, has given us new insight into some of the secrets of ancient Egypt, and who knows what else remains to be discovered?

PETER LACOVARA

Archaeologist specializing in the material culture of ancient Egypt and Nubia. He graduated from the Oriental Institute of the University of Chicago and is the senior curator of ancient Egyptian, Nubian, and Near Eastern art at the Michael C. Carlos Museum at Emory University in Atlanta.

THE PYRAMID AT MEIDUM
The collapsed pyramid at Meidum (to the southeast of Cairo), was originally tiered, but the Emperor Snefru converted it into the first pyramid with smooth sides. His son, Khufu, would later build the Great Pyramid of Giza.

The Dynasties of the Ancient Land of the Nile

More than 4,000 years of unequaled stability made Egypt into a great power of the ancient world and a model for future kingdoms. Due to Egypt's antiquity, the pharaohs are responsible for hundreds of enigmas yet to be resolved

E gypt is a gift from the Nile. This was the view of the Greek historian and traveler Herodotus (484–425 BCE), author of the monumental *Histories*, the first notable historical record in the ancient world. To a rational and practical man like him, a stranger to belief in the afterlife and metempsychosis, Egypt was merely "the country that the Nile watered with its floods and the Egyptians were those who live downstream from the city of Elephantine and drink water from that river." Herodotus could not have imagined how with this succinct description he would open the doors to a land full of marvels to be discovered by posterity.

From the first waterfall to the south of Elephantine, through the lands of Nubia, to the estuary in the Mediterranean Sea, the waters of the Nile River

brought life to an extraordinary and long-lived civilization. Before the time of the pharaohs, a wave of nomads from North Africa who practiced agriculture and domesticated animals had settled on the riverbanks and the nearby oases. These somewhat dark times, known as Dynasty Zero (5550–3100 BCE) and dominated by the Horus kings, led to the Early Dynastic Period (3100–2686 BCE), when the country of the Two Lands, Lower Egypt to the north and Upper Egypt to the south, were unified under the first pharaoh. While we know Egyptians considered the beginning of creation took place in the waters of Nun, the identity of the first bearer of the "double crown" is not as clear. The discovery of a clay tablet and a limestone hammer at Hierakonpolis in 1897 led to Narmer, King of Upper Egypt, being credited as the first Pharaoh. Some Egyptologists have suggested Aha, his child

and successor, as a candidate. There are some who have said that Narmer and Aha were the same person. He may in any case have had two names: the official one and that of Men or Menes, the founder of Memphis, the first capital of unified Egypt.

NARMER, THE UNIFIER

In 1985, a team from the German Archaeological Institute led by Günter Dreyer, which worked in the necropolis of Umm el-Qaab close to Abydos, seem to have put an end to the confusion after finding a seal printed on a vessel which included the names of the first eight pharaohs. It listed Narmer at the beginning, followed by Aha. In 1997, at this same burial site from the time of Dynasty Zero and the first two dynasties of the Early Period, Dreyer discovered clay vessels and tablets with inscriptions, possibly proof of the most ancient writing system known, even older than the cuneiform of

RAMESSES II
Monumental sculptures of the
powerful Pharaoh Ramesses
II at the entrance to the rock-
carved temple at Abu Simbel.

Mesopotamia, in the tomb of Scorpion I (3200 BCE).

In the Old Kingdom (2686–2134 BCE), Zoser, the second pharaoh of the Third Dynasty, ordered the first tiered pyramid to be built in Saqqara, the biggest necropolis in Memphis. The beginning of the next dynasty featured the perfect architecture of Snefru (2613–2589 BCE), who built several pyramids in Meidum and Dahshur, where highlights include the Rhomboid Pyramid and the North Pyramid (the second largest in Egypt). His successor, Khufu – in Greek, Cheops – ruled for 23 years, approximately the same amount of time that it took to build the Great Pyramid of Giza. Its square base, 479 ft high (145 m), with over two million limestone blocks have made it the pinnacle of all monuments. The other two pyramids of Giza, somewhat less grand, were built during the reign of Khafra – Chephren in Greek (2558–2532 BCE) – and Menkaure – Mykerinos in Greek (2532–2503 BCE)–. The mathematical relationship between the faces of the pyramid and its height held to an enigmatic "golden mean." Beside the Temple of Khafra, the image of the Great Sphinx was sculpted: a monumental figure with the body of a lion and a human head. Pyramid fever, evident in Abusir and Saqqara, lessened as the Old Kingdom progressed. The Pyramid Texts – inscriptions on the walls of the antechamber and the burial chamber first appeared in the Pyramid of Unas (2375–2345 BCE), Unas being the fourth

and last ruler of the Fifth Dynasty. These texts describe rituals, legends and incantations to help the pharaoh face his travel to the beyond.

The reigns of Teti and Pepi, in the Sixth Dynasty, marked the end of the Old Kingdom and the beginning of the First Intermediate Period (2134–2030 BCE). During this period there were over 25 rulers in 50 years (from the Seventh and Eighth Dynasties), which led to the division of the country between two kingdoms, Herakleopolis in the north and Thebes in the south, and several other city-states.

THE MIDDLE KINGDOM

Around 2030 BCE, Pharaoh Mentuhotep from the Eleventh Theban Dynasty contributed to the fall of the Tenth Dynasty of Herakleopolis, as well as unify the Two Lands again, begin the Middle Kingdom and turn Thebes into the new capital. He erected his burial temple at Deir el-Bahri. It was a golden age during which there was internal peace and prosperity, though there were military campaigns against Libya, Palestine and Nubia, with the aim of expanding Egypt's borders,

obtaining minerals – particularly gold – and controlling trade routes. Senusret I, the second pharaoh of the Twelfth Dynasty, is responsible for the construction of the white chapel at Karnak, famous for its reliefs and two red granite obelisks at Heliopolis, one of which is still standing and is the oldest of those preserved in Egypt.

After the death of the Queen-Pharaoh Sobekneferu (1799–1795 BCE), the Middle Kingdom entered a spiral of brief reigns up until the Second Intermediate Period (1640–1539 BCE), marked by

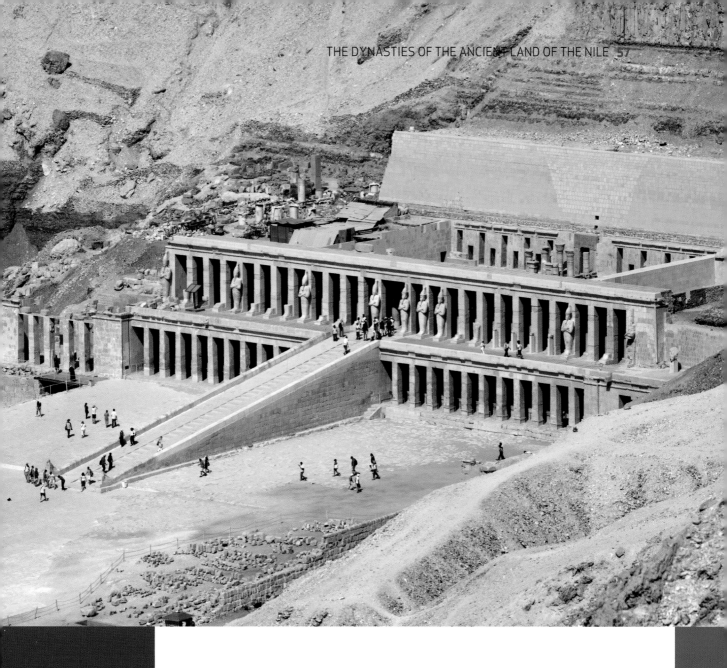

THE DYNASTIES OF THE ANCIENT LAND OF THE NILE

TIERED PYRAMID
The work of Pharaoh Zoser.
It is the oldest monument
carved out of stone in the
history of humanity.

**TEMPLE OF
HATSHEPSUT**
Located in the valley of
Deir el-Bahri, it is thought
to have been designed by
the architect Senenmut
with whom, it seems, the
queen-pharaoh conceived
her daughter Neferure.

the invasion of the Hyksos,
eastern immigrants from
Canaan. Their kings established the capital at Avaris,
at the Nile delta, from where
they governed Lower and
Middle Egypt and introduced
the horse, war chariots and
bronze smelting.

THE NEW KINGDOM'S SPLENDOR
Ahmose I threw out the Hyksos, founded the Seventeenth
Dynasty of the New Kingdom
(1539–1075 BCE) and established the capital of the Two
Lands at Thebes again. It
seems that the pyramid that
he ordered built in Abydos

may have been the last one
from the time of Ancient
Egypt.
With Pharaoh Thutmose I
(1504–1492 BCE), the third
king of the Seventeenth
Dynasty, the borders of the
country extended to the third
waterfall in Nubia and the
banks of the Euphrates in
Mesopotamia. This monarch
ordered that the Temple of
Karnak, located to the north
of Thebes and dedicated to
the main deity Amun-Ra, be
enlarged. He also decided to
build his tomb in the Valley of
the Kings, near the desert hills
west of Thebes. His was the

first one of the New Kingdom.
From then on, the traditional
pyramid burial complex,
which was also the object of
plundering by grave robbers,
was replaced by the hypogeum, carved into a mountain-
side. When Thutmose II died,
one of his children – Thutmose
III – born of one pf his secondary wives, inherited the title of
pharaoh. When Thutmose III
was still a baby, Hatshepsut
(1503–1482 BCE), who was
"great royal wife" of his father,
became co-regent.
The queen, supported by the
senior official and royal architect Senenmut (1473–1458

Continued on page 60 ▶

The Egypt of the Pharaohs

5,000 years ago, on the banks of the Nile, one of the most sophisticated and long-lasting civilizations of ancient times began. Its sovereign rulers, known as pharaohs, built kingdoms and left one-of-a-kind architectural remains.

The Two Great Capitals

Located in the delta of the Nile and founded by Narmer (or Menes), Memphis was the capital of Egypt for a thousand years until, in 2050 BC, the title was taken from it by Thebes, the cradle of the Eleventh Dynasty, which reunified Egypt and founded the Middle Kingdom. Thebes retained its status as capital throughout the entire New Kingdom. In some periods, both cities shared the status of capital: Memphis, the political; Thebes, the religious.

MAIN SITES

The Nile valley is replete with ruins from Ancient Egypt, the fruit of three thousand years of history. The most well-known archaeological sites in order of antiquity are: the pre-dynastic city of Abydos, site of the Great Temple of Osiris and the oldest royal cemetery in the world; Memphis, with the necropolis of Dahshur, Saqqara, and Giza, which house the pyramids; Thebes, with the temples of Karnak, and Luxor and the Valley of the Kings.

PHARAOHS AND MONUMENTS

1 Zoser
(2665-2645 BC) Third Dynasty

During his reign, he built the first stone funeral complex in the world: the tiered pyramid of Saqqara.

2 Khufu
(2579-2556 BC) Fourth Dynasty

He ordered the Great Pyramid of Giza, his mausoleum, to be built. He was the father of the Pharaoh Khafra and the grandfather of Menkaure, the other great sovereign builders of the pyramids of Giza.

3 Ramesses II
(1290-1224 BC) Nineteenth Dynasty

Pharaoh, warrior and builder. He led the famous battle of Qadesh against the Hittite Empire. He built many colossal statues, built the temples of Abu Simbel and Ramesseum, and founded the city of Pi-Ramesses (Tanis), his capital.

MEDITERRANEAN SEA

Alexandria

Pyramids of Giza

Heliopolis

Giza **2**

Saqqara **1**

○ **Memphis**

Tiered pyramid

● Dahshur

LOWER EGYPT

Herakleopolis ●

Eastern Desert

4 Tell el-Amarna

Amarna Letters

Western Desert

EGYPT

Abydos ●

Nile River

Deir el-Bahri

Valley of the Kings **5**

● Karnak

○ **Thebes**

Enlarged area

6

Colossi of Memnon

UPP EGY

N

0   Miles   125

Abu Simbel **3**

Why did Thutmose III erase the name of his aunt, Hatshepsut, from her monuments?

When it was discovered that the name of the Queen-Pharaoh Hatshepsut had been erased from her monuments. Egyptologists thought it was due to the vengeance of her nephew, Thutmose III, who had been sent away for "usurping" the throne. However, this theory has been deemed invalid as the defacing began 20 years after the death of Hatshepsut. Currently, it is thought that this occurred due to inheritance or dynastic issues among her family.

nigmas

4 Akhenaten
(1353-1336 BC) Seventeenth Dynasty

The son of Amenhotep III was the greatest religious reformer of Ancient Egypt, enforcing the monotheistic worship of Aten. He installed his capital at Tell el-Amarna.

Nefertiti
(1353-1340 BC) Eighteenth Dynasty

She was the great royal wife of Akhenaten, who made her co-regent. Some Egyptologists suspect that she inspired the religious schism promoted by her husband.

5 Thutmose I
(1504-1492 BC) Eighteenth Dynasty

He extended the kingdom to Upper Nubia and waged war on the banks of the Euphrates. He was the founder of the royal Theban necropolis of the Valley of the Kings.

Hatshepsut
(1479-1457 BC) Eighteenth Dynasty

Heiress of Thutmose I, she was the most powerful Egyptian queen-pharaoh. She ordered the Temple of Djeser-Djeseru, one of the greatest architectural gems of Ancient Egypt, to be built.

Thutmose III
(1457-1425 BC) Eighteenth Dynasty

Called "the Great," he was responsible for the greatest territorial expansion of the Egyptian kingdom. He subjugated the kingdoms of the Middle East and the Eastern Mediterranean. He built the Temple of Amun-Ra at Karnak.

Tutankhamun
(1332-1323 BC)
Eighteenth Dynasty

The son of Akhenaten, he restored the worship of Amun. He is the most well-known pharaoh as a result of the discovery of his intact hypogeum in 1922 in the Valley of the Kings.

6 Amenhotep III
(1390-1353 BC) Eighteenth Dynasty

His rule was distinguished by the most construction during the time of a single pharaoh in Ancient Egypt. The Colossi of Memnon are the remains of the fabulous temple that was built next to the Nile.

CHRONOLOGY OF ANCIENT EGYPT

NAME	YEARS	DYNASTIES
Early Period	3100 BC -2686 BC	I and II
Old Kingdom	2686 BC -2134 BC.	III, IV, V and VI
First Intermediate Period	2134 BC -2030 BC	VII, VIII, IX, X and XI
Middle Kingdom	2030 BC -1640 BC	XI and XII
Second Intermediate Period	1640 BC -1539 BC	XIII, XIV, XV, XVI and XVII
New Kingdom	1539 BC -1075 BC	XVIII, XIX and XX
Third Intermediate Period	1075 BC -650 BC	XXI, XXII, XXIII, XXIV and XXV
Late Period	650 BC -332 BC	XXVI, XXVII, XXVIII, XXIX, XXX and XXXI
Hellenistic Period	332 BC -30 BC	

THE CENTURIES-OLD CULTURE OF THE NILE

The civilization of Ancient Egypt extends approximately from 3200 BC to the death of Cleopatra VII in 30 BC. Conventionally, its history begins with King Narmer, who joined Upper and Lower Egypt and founded the first dynasty. Egyptian history is divided into three high periods –Old Kingdom, Middle Kingdom, and New Kingdom. The height of its splendor was during the Fourth, Eighteenth, and Nineteenth dynasties. The Persian conquest in the sixth century BC marked the empire's final decline.

BCE), who may have also been her lover, assumed absolute power as pharaoh and started to be represented as a man. One of the milestones of her reign was the commercial expedition by land and sea to the Land of Punt. In exchange for typical Egyptian products, likely necklaces, beads and weapons, they obtained ebony, ivory, gold, and above all, frankincense trees – source of the resinous substance which was burned in religious ceremonies. The details of the expedition are preserved on the walls of the Temple of Hatshepsut in Deir el-Bahri, though no one knows for certain where Punt, the mythical place, is to be found. Perhaps Ethiopia or Eritrea.

In the shadow of Hatshepsut, Thutmose III learned the role of pharaoh, which he was able to exercise with the spirit of a conqueror when he was 21 years old. The military incursions of this ruler, described as the "Egyptian Napoleon," seemed infinite. All were successful judging by the Annals of Thutmose III recorded on the walls of the Temple of Amun-Ra at Karnak, which were a faithful reflection of the expedition diaries, the work of his scribes. His regime of conquest made him, as the sole king of the Two Lands, into the principal power of the Near East, Nubia (to the fourth waterfall), Syria-Palestine, Libya, and the Phoenician coast were all within the borders of his kingdom. Using his political pragmatism, he was known for bringing the princes of the conquered countries to Egypt so that they might know the greatness of its culture and learn to be loyal to the pharaonic kingdom. Thutmose III, the conqueror, who ruled up to 1425 BCE, also took on large architectural projects. In addition to a large number of temples and monuments, the festival hall and the red chapel at Karnak were notable. He also erected seven large obelisks, the golden points of which reflected the light of the sun. Four of them were later moved to city squares in Rome, Istanbul, London, and New York. New excavations in the funeral temple of Thutmose at Luxor–connected to Karnak by an avenue of sphinxes and far from his tomb in the Valley of the Kings – revealed that he had built on top of an ancient necropolis with four levels of tombs below.

THE SCHISM OF AKHENATEN

The New Kingdom turned to the worship of Aten, represented by a sun disk. This religion came on the scene for the first time in the Temple of Heliopolis during the rule of Amenhotep II (1427–1400 BCE) – likely the pharaoh mentioned in the Book of Exodus in the Bible – and then continued during the reign of Amenhotep III (1390–1353 BCE). However, it was his successor, Amenhotep IV (1353–1336 BCE), who proclaimed Aten the only god of Egypt and prohibited the worship of Amun-Ra. In the fifth year of his rule, Amenhotep IV changed his name to Akhenaten and founded a new capital named Akhetaten (Tell el-Amarna). His great royal wife was Nefertiti, reputed to be very beautiful and mysterious, and who had such an important political and religious role that she was sometimes represented wearing the crown of the pharaoh. After the death of Akhenaten, the mysterious Smenkhare briefly assumed pharaonic power. Some Egyptologists believe Nefertiti disguised herself under this name. What is certain is that all of them, including Aten, seem to have been erased from Egyptian memory with one stroke, from the moment a nine-year-old boy named Tutankhamun (1332–1323 BCE) became pharaoh. He was the son of Akhenaten, and his royal government was run by the Grand Vizier Ay and Army Commander Horemheb. Centuries later, after his tomb was found nearly intact in 1922, Tutankhamun became the "golden boy" of Ancient Egypt and continues to be an endless source of surprises and mysteries.

DECADENCE AND INVASIONS

Most notable in the Ramesside Period of the Nineteenth and Twentieth Dynasties is the military Pharaoh Ramesses II (1290–1224 BCE). This ruler was responsible for the legendary battle against the Hittites at

◀ *Continued from page 57*

Continued on page 64 ▶

Christiane Desroches-Noblecourt
1913–2011

Eminent and lauded French Egyptologist who was appointed to the Egyptian Antiquities Department of the Louvre Museum and was the first woman to lead an excavation in Egypt. She dedicated her life to studying and protecting the pharaonic heritage, and especially to saving the temples of Abu Simbel and other Egyptian monuments in Nubia from flooding, when threatened by the Aswan Dam. She was the author of numerous publications on Ancient Egypt, the reign of Ramesses II, and the role of women in the time of the pharaohs.

COMMITTED. She gained international acclaim for her resolute campaign to protect the temples of Abu Simbel.

Nicholas Reeves
1956

With a doctorate from Durham in 1984, this British Egyptologist and curator of the departments of Egyptian Art at the British Museum, the New York Metropolitan Museum of Art, and other private collections, is known for his research in the Valley of Kings. In the year 2000, along with his colleague Geoffrey T. Martin, he discovered an unexplored underground chamber while trying to find the tombs of the queens of the Seventeenth Dynasty. This was chamber KV63, later explored by the American Egyptologist Otto J. Schaden. It is a mummification room which contained coffins and jars, but no mummy.

VALLEY OF THE KINGS. Reeves maintains that the tombs of the queens of the Seventeenth Dynasty (never found) would be beside those of their husbands.

Zahi Hawass

This famous Egyptian archaeologist is among the Egyptologists who have unraveled the most mysteries regarding Ancient Egypt in recent decades. He graduated with a degree in Greek and Roman Archaeology when he was 19 years old. The discovery of new passages in the Great Pyramid are among his findings. In 2005, he led the computed tomography (CT) of the mummy of Tutankhamun, which made it possible to discern the causes of his early death. In recent years, Hawass has focused on identifying the mummies in the Valley of the Kings, using new medical technologies. Thanks to these, the mummies of queens Hatshepsut and Tiye (the wife of Amenhotep III and the mother of Pharaoh Akhenaten) were identified. Advances in genetics have also permitted him to discover the mother of the famous Pharaoh Tutankhamun and the skeleton of his father – which Hawass claims is Akhenaten – among the previously unidentified mummies from the Seventeenth Dynasty.

RECOGNITION. In his role as head of the Supreme Council of Antiquities and as minister, Hawass worked hard to return the treasures of Ancient Egypt, that had been spread throughout the world, to their country of origin.

1947

"As scientists, we must have an open mind, but our ideas about the past have to be based on archaeological evidence." Z. H.

Mark Lehner
1950

This American archaeologist and Egyptologist is the foremost expert on the plateau of Giza. He received his doctorate from Yale University in 1990 with the dissertation "Archaeology of an Image: The Great Sphinx of Giza." Mark Lehner is notable because of his comprehensive and multidisciplinary research on the pharaonic area of Giza, which he has mapped and analyzed. His thorough work led him to discover the pyramid workers' city and to make new discoveries about the pyramids and other monuments of the famous Egyptian plateau.

GREAT SPHINX. Attracted from a young age to this monument thanks to the esoteric theories of Edgar Cayce, Lehner is one of the Egyptologists to go deepest into its mysteries.

The Great Sphinx of Giza

To the east of the pyramid of Khafra stands the Great Sphinx, the greatest and oldest of all statues carved by man. This colossal figure of a lion with a human head is as fascinating and enigmatic to Egyptologists today as it was to the last pharaohs of ancient Egypt.

Sentinel and Protector

The Sphinx was carved in limestone from the quarry of the Great Pyramid. Its construction is attributed to Khafra. The head, supposedly a portrait of said pharaoh, was carved into a hard layer of rock, while the body was sculpted in softer stone and thus has eroded more. For centuries the colossal figure was covered by desert sand and over the course of history it has been repaired using masonry. It was created as a lookout figure, part of the Khafra funerary complex, and it would have been considered to exercise the function of sentinel and protector of the sacred grounds of Giza.

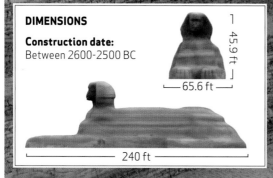

DIMENSIONS

Construction date:
Between 2600-2500 BC

45.9 ft

65.6 ft

240 ft

Missing Nose
The fifteenth-century Arab chronicles report that the face of the Great Sphinx was defaced at that time by Mamluks.

Stele
The stele of Thutmose IV, or the Dream Stele, is slab of granite a 7 ft tall, weighing several tons. It is partially damaged. It once cited Khafra as the builder of the Sphinx, but that piece of text has not been preserved.

Who Defaced the Nose of the Great Sphinx?

Tradition attributes the removal of the nose of the Great Sphinx to Napoleon's soldiers, but there is Egyptian documentation from the fifteenth century that attributes the deed to an iconoclastic movement led by the fanatic Sufi Mohamed Sa'im al-Dahr. Noting that the peasants made offerings to the large statue, this enemy of pagan manifestations attacked the sphinx in 1389 and destroyed its nose. He was lynched for doing this.

nigmas

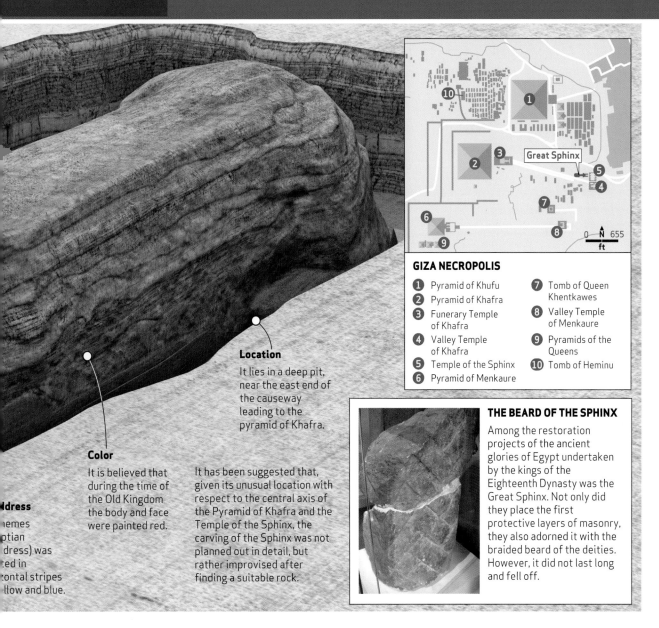

GIZA NECROPOLIS

1. Pyramid of Khufu
2. Pyramid of Khafra
3. Funerary Temple of Khafra
4. Valley Temple of Khafra
5. Temple of the Sphinx
6. Pyramid of Menkaure
7. Tomb of Queen Khentkawes
8. Valley Temple of Menkaure
9. Pyramids of the Queens
10. Tomb of Heminu

Great Sphinx

0 N 655 ft

Location
It lies in a deep pit, near the east end of the causeway leading to the pyramid of Khafra.

Color
It is believed that during the time of the Old Kingdom the body and face were painted red.

ddress
nemes
ptian
dress) was
ted in
ontal stripes
llow and blue.

It has been suggested that, given its unusual location with respect to the central axis of the Pyramid of Khafra and the Temple of the Sphinx, the carving of the Sphinx was not planned out in detail, but rather improvised after finding a suitable rock.

THE BEARD OF THE SPHINX

Among the restoration projects of the ancient glories of Egypt undertaken by the kings of the Eighteenth Dynasty was the Great Sphinx. Not only did they place the first protective layers of masonry, they also adorned it with the braided beard of the deities. However, it did not last long and fell off.

SPHINX AS SEEN BY THE WEST

1615	1681	1755	1798	1838	1858	1887	1925
rge Sandys	Cornelis de Bruinj	Frederic Norden	Vivant Denon	David Roberts	Francis Frith	Henri Béchard	Émile Baraize

From Plundering to Archaeology

The jewels and other luxurious items amassed inside the tombs of the pharaohs attracted tomb robbers as early as the time of the Old Kingdom. In the New Kingdom, so as to prevent pillaging, hypogeum were excavated in the Valley of the Kings and a town was founded nearby – Deir el-Medina – where workers, scribes, foremen, and their families watched over the tombs so that nothing would disturb the peace of the deceased kings. Despite the efforts of the pharaohs, as early as in the rule of Ramesses IX (1127–1108 BCE), there were recorded cases of employees who let the tombs be plundered in exchange for part of the loot. At the end of the New Kingdom, the tomb robbers, among them a group of priests of Amun, stripped the Theban necropolis, leaving the majority of mummies in only their cloth wrappings. Plundering did not stop there, and the greed of the robbers extended to the mummies themselves,

AUGUSTE MARIETTE
The French archaeologist Auguste Mariette (center), defender of the integrity of Egyptian treasure, at an excavation of Saqqara.

whose remains they used to make remarkable powders for the superstitious rulers of Europe and Asia.
In the nineteenth century, hundreds of adventurers satisfied the hunger of the learned Europeans collectors and the continent's museums for the treasures of Ancient Egypt. The alternative to plundering came after archeology took root among the European sciences. In 1835, the Egyptian Antiquities Service

was created to protect the treasures and monuments of Ancient Egypt from both domestic and foreign plundering. In 1881 Frenchman Gaston Maspero, director of this service, was able to enter tomb DB320 of Deir el-Bahri, in which the family of Abdel-Rassoul, the most prolific raiders of the tombs of Egypt, had uncovered 40 mummies, nine pharaohs among them. Maspero prevented their dispersion.

A European Plunderer

The Italian adventurer Giovanni Battista Belzoni first settled in Great Britain, then headed to Alexandria in 1815. Like a bulldozer, he invaded the depths of Ancient Egypt, with the support of the British consul. His main targets were Abu Simbel—which he cleared sand from and found the larger temple of Ramesses II—and the Valley of the Kings. He shipped the monumental bust of Ramesses II to the British Museum, and also sent the obelisk of Ptolemy IX and the alabaster sarcophagus of Seti I to London.

BELZONI
Depiction of Belzoni, an individual of considerable physical presence, dressed in Egyptian clothing.

Kadesh, recorded in detail on tablets and resolved after signing a peace treaty – which was the first in history between two great powers. He had his accomplishments described triumphantly on the pillars of his colossal funeral temple, the Ramesseum, in Thebes. On the banks of the Nile, he left an extraordinary architectural legacy: two rock-cut temples at Abu Simbel, one dedicated to himself and the other to his wife

◀ Continued from page 60

Nefertari. These were elevated to higher ground in the 1960s due to the construction of the Aswan Dam. Ramesses III (1184–1153 BCE) led Egypt in the greatly celebrated victory of the pharaonic army over the Sea Peoples, a coalition of peoples from around the Aegean Sea who tried to invade Egypt. That battle is engraved in the reliefs of his funeral temple at Medinet Habu, to the west of Thebes. It was the swan song of the New Kingdom, which started to languish and then ended after the death of Ramesses XI.

Pharaonic Egypt continued to decline in the Third Intermediate Period (1075–650 BCE). Rulers included the priests of Amun and the Libyans. The Late Period (650–332 BCE), under the native Saite Dynasty, was controlled by Nubians, Assyrians and Persians. However, Egypt seemed to be reborn when Macedonian Alexander the Great ended Persian rule and was crowned pharaoh (332–331 BCE). He hardly ruled for a year, but during that time he founded the city of Alexandria. A brief period of rule by the Macedonian Dynasty was followed by the Ptolemaic Dynasty beginning in 305 BCE. The enigmatic Cleopatra VII was the last queen of Egypt (51–30 BCE), ruling amidst the hegemonic power of imperial Rome.

HYPOSTYLE HALL
The pillared hall of the Great Temple of Karnak, with smooth papyrus columns, was built during the rule of Amenhotep III.

Decline and Recovery

The strength of the Egyptian society of the New Kingdom is evident. Half a century after Akhenaten's religious revolution, Egypt recovered its prestige thanks to Seti I who re-conquered the territories that were lost in the Middle East during the confused and troubled reign of the heretical pharaoh.

Akhenaten's Capital

The repression campaign against the monotheism begun by Akhenaten must have been relentless, judging by the few vestiges of Akhetaten (Tell el-Amarna, in image). The capital built by the heretical pharaoh was dismantled and condemned to oblivion by the powerful priests of Amun and virtually disappeared into the desert sands.

INSCRIPTIONS Hieroglyphic inscriptions recorded in stone in the magnificent palace of Seti I at Abydos.

Were the Pharaohs Black?

The origin of the kings of ancient Egypt is yet to be resolved by Egyptologists. There are defenders of the theory that the pharaohs were black, and there are those who maintain they had Caucasian origins. Neither theory is provable.

After a great deal of research undertaken on this subject, it seems that the only black pharaohs of ancient Egypt were Nubians from the kingdom of Napata, who began to rule in Egypt toward the end of the Third Intermediate Period during a time of Libyan dominance. Piye, a pharaoh of Nubian descent, founded the dynasty known as the "Kushite" in Thebes in 747 BCE. This was followed by the reigns of Shabaka, Shebitku and Taharqa, which barely make up a century of black identity, which ended with the invasion of the Assyrians in 664 BCE. The Kushite kings reinstated the funerary tradition of the pyramids in Nubia. With the exception of Taharqa, who built the largest pyramid at Nuri, the other black pharaohs were buried in the burial chambers of the pyramid of El-Kurru.

There is no doubt about the geographical Africanness of ancient Egypt. But insofar as most of the features, habits and customs of ancient Egyptians, it's another story. While in 1899 French archaeologist Émile Amélineau concluded that "the populations that settled in the Nile valley were black, considering the legends about the black-red goddess Isis," in the twentieth century some anthropologists emphasized the physical link of the Egyptians with the people of Europe and southern Asia as opposed to sub-Saharan Africa. Afrocentrism advocates opposed the version in which the Egyptians appeared as Caucasian or Indo-European. Afrocentrists had no doubts about the black identity of the rulers of ancient Egypt, once called Kemet or Kermit (the Black Land) by its inhabitants and linked to the kingdoms of Nubia and Ethiopia. According to them, Eurocentrism had buried the Egyptian reality. In support of their theory, they presented black African examples, such as the Great Sphinx of Giza and the contents of the tomb of Mesehti, a senior official of the Eleventh Dynasty of the Middle Kingdom in Asyut: forty painted wooden statuettes representing a group of Nubian archers. And Queen Tiye, to whom her husband Pharaoh Amenhotep III consecrated the temple of Sedeinga, located in Nubia between the second and third waterfalls of the Nile, has been included in the category of black Egypt. Regarding these conflicting positions, American anthropologist Charles Loring Brace has pointed out that "attempts to force the classification of Egyptians as black or white has no biological justification."

Company of negro archers marching in fours from the tomb of an officer Nasahti. The coffin on one side and the boat on the other, are from the same tomb.

Une compagnie d'infanterie légère, formée de quarante hommes.
Company of light infantry forty strong.

enigmas

WAS THERE A RED-HAIRED PHARAOH?

In his book *The Spirit of the Laws*, the Baron of Montesquieu, speaking against the slavery of blacks and differences based on race, said that the ancient Egyptians, "the greatest philosophers in the world," had exterminated any red-haired person that fell into their hands. Red-haired people were identified with the infernal god Seth (Set), murderer of the benefactor Osiris, and they were considered a sign of misery and misfortune for the family with a red-headed child. In light of these beliefs, it is surprising that, according to recent evidence, Ramesses II was red-haired, as was his father Seti I, whose name also refers to the "lord of darkness." It is likely that the Ramesside lineage included a Libyan-Berber ascendant – a population with a high percentage of redheads – enlisted in the pharaonic army as an archer under the orders of Horemheb, the last pharaoh of the Eighteenth Dynasty. The scientific finding of Horemheb's red hairs is also evidence that some cruel customs of the Egyptians must have changed over time.

Symbols of Power

The continuity of the symbols of power over three thousand years of monarchy highlights the stability and traditionalism of ancient Egyptian society. With few exceptions, the crowns, scepters, and other objects that symbolized power repeat dynasty after dynasty.

Crowns

In ancient Egypt, the crown served a dual political and religious role. That is also why the gods are often depicted with a crown, a symbol of their authority over humans. Before unification, the sovereigns of Lower Egypt were distinguished from those of Upper Egypt by their crowns, each relating to a patron god. The white crown of Upper Egypt was associated with the vulture goddess Nekhbet, and the red crown of Lower Egypt was associated with the snake goddess Wadjet. The fusion of the two crowns resulted in the double or Sejemty crown, symbol of the authority of the pharaoh over the "Two Lands." Beginning in the New Kingdom period, the crown served to distinguish the dynastic origin of the king. Aside from the royal one, there were also other crowns for strictly ceremonial or religious use.

HEDJET
This was shaped like an oblong turban and represented the monarchs of Upper Egypt. This was the crown of the Theban dynasties.

KHEPRESH
The blue crown had a liturgical use. The pharaohs used it during the offerings to the gods.

DESHERET
It is red, cylindrical, with an upward extending "arm" and a rounded bulge at the front, connected with the bee, the symbol of dynasties. It was the crown of Lower Egypt.

SHUTY
Made up of two long feathers, this is the crown of the god Amun. It also symbolizes the union of the Two Lands. In the New Kingdom they were worn by women of the royal house and some priestesses.

ATEF
This was also a ceremonial cro[wn] for religious use. It was relate[d] to the god Osiris and the god Herishef, with the head of a ra[m]

Crowns and Materials

One of the most surprising things to archae-ologists was not finding any royal crown. Given this absence, experts speculated about the quality of the materials with which the first crowns were manufactured, such as wood, ivory or papyrus. However, after the appearance of bronze, it is believed that the sejemty crown or the "Double Crown of the Two Lands" (pictured to the left) became, as in today's monarchies, a precious treasure that was bequeathed as an inheritance and only used on coronation day.

Emblems of Authority

The supreme authority of the monarch was not only signified by the crown. Emblems, scepters, dia-dems, headdresses and other lux-urious accessories were part of an extensive dowry that was used by the king and his family to keep his subjects at a reverential distance. In the representation of power, the scepters held a special relevance.

Each one had a particular meaning related to the actions of govern-ment or religious content, and they were full of symbolism. Thus, the heka staff and nejej whip, while indicating the functions of guidance and justice, respectively also iden-tified the pharaoh with the mighty god Osiris, mythical bearer of these ruling instruments.

RITUAL BEARD
This false beard was used by the pharaoh on signifi-cant occasions. It identified him with Osiris, the legendary founder of Egypt.

COSTLINESS
As seen in the example of these sandals belon-ging to Tutankhamen, costliness was the com-mon denominator of all royal attire.

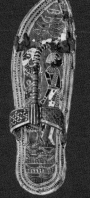

NEMES
A cloth headdress that took the place of the crown during the daily activities of the pharaoh. It was held to the head with a headband.

URAEUS
It was the representation of Wadjet, the cobra goddess and protector of the pharaohs, the only people permitted to wear it on their clothing.

"SEJEM" SCEPTER
Symbolized strength and the magical power of the king, his family and the nobility. The image shows Queen Nefertari with the sejem.

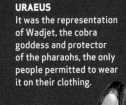

DIADEM
These served to display royal dig-nity with or without the nemes. They were particularly used, as in the case of the one above, by the sons of the pharaoh.

STAFF AND WHIP
The heka staff and nejej whip are emblems of royalty. These pastoral instruments designate the pharaoh as leader of his people.

What Occurred with Akhenaten and Nefertiti?

The Pharaoh Akhenaten and his wife, the beautiful Nefertiti, have gone down in history as a couple in love. Together they led a religious revolution, and then the queen suddenly disappeared without a trace.

Akhenaten and Nefertiti were one of the most famous couples of ancient Egypt. However, the story of the heretic king and his beloved wife is full of mysteries. Akhenaten was the second son of Amenhotep II and his Great Royal Wife, Tiye. Raised by his mother, who was not of royal lineage but was the daughter of a high nobleman of the court of Thutmose IV, he was introduced to the worship of Aten, a "new" divinity with great prestige within the royal family.

The pharaoh sought to promote the worship of this new god and to reduce the power that was held by the priests of Amun, the most popular of the Egyptian gods in the New Kingdom, credited for driving out the Hyksos. Due to the gifts of the faithful, the clergy had become wealthy and powerful enough to pose a threat, even capable of interfering in the royal succession. To avoid this, during the fifth year of his rule Amenhotep IV began a religious revolution. He imposed the worship of Aten (represented by the sun disk), changed his name to Akhenaten ("the one who benefits Aten") and proclaimed himself high priest, the only mediator between men and the new supreme god. Furthermore, blatantly emphasizing the schism, he left Thebes and founded a new city further north and called it Akhetaten ("the horizon of Aten") and moved the court there. This location is now called Tell el-Amarna. He also started a new artistic style, more naturalistic, familiar, and intimate moving away from the traditional hieratic representations of kings, which was inconceivable in ancient Egypt.

His Great Royal Wife, Nefertiti ("The beautiful has arrived"), the best-known Egyptian queen due to the famous bust that portrays her, played a prominent role in the establishment of the new religion, to the point that the schism was attributed to her. Judging by the archaeological findings, her political and religious importance were extraordinary. She was given the name Neferneferuaten ("The most perfect of Aten's perfections") and was even represented with a club in hand slaughtering enemies – an image reserved exclusively for pharaohs–and in ceremonial scenes on an equal footing with her husband. She also had temples exclusively for the worship of Aten, such as Hut-Benben.

MYSTERIOUS NEFERTITI

Unlike the pharaoh, Nefertiti's origins are obscure. Some authors believe that she was

enigmas

WAS PHARAOH AKHENATON A HERMAPHRODITE?

The effeminate appearance of the sculptures of Akhenaten (below) has often raised this issue, but it has not been confirmed. Although he is depicted with feminine traits—gynecomastia, and broad thighs and hips—various medical conditions have also been attributed to him such as Marfan or Fröhlich Syndrome, Egyptologists are inclined to think that his artistic representation underwent a change, linked to the eminent role of Nefertiti in the establishment of the worship of Aten. It is possible that the affinity with his wife led to the creation of an androgynous representation signifying a compendium of the divine couple.

OFFERING
Akhenaten and Nefertiti making an offering to the god Aten, in a relief found at Tell el-Amarna.

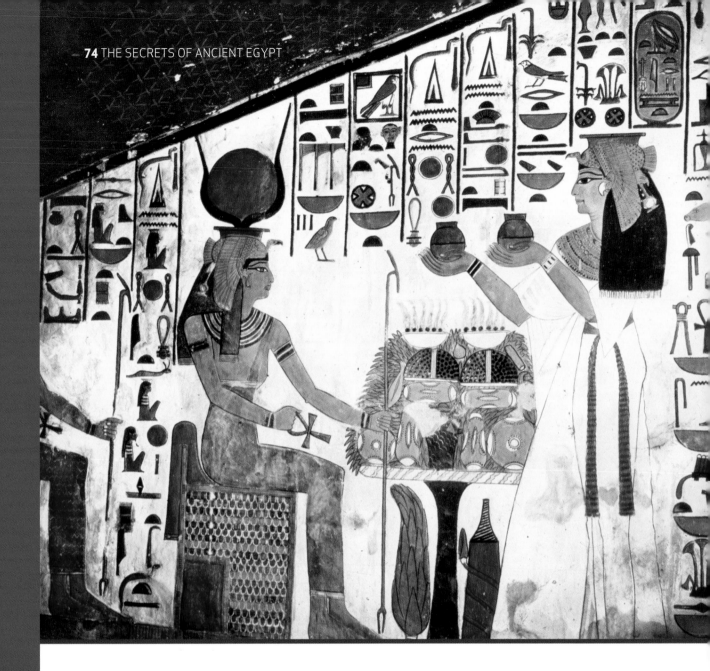

a Mitanni princess. Others believe that she was the daughter of Ay, brother of Tiye, Akhenaten's mother. Either way, based on the images passed down to us, her marriage to the pharaoh – with whom she had six daughters – was a happy one, at least until the twelfth year of his reign. From that year onward, the prominence of Nefertiti decays and records of her soon completely disappears. A painful event, likely the death of Meketaten, the second of the daughters of the royal couple, must have prece-ded this rapid eclipse. Shortly after that tragic event came the death of Tiye, Akhenaten's beloved mother.

DISAPPEARANCE AND DISCOVERIES
Confronted with the sudden disappearance of the Queen, Egyptologists hold several theories among them. The first and simplest is that Nefertiti died the following year. That would be why the king married his and his lovely wife's oldest daughter, Merita-ten. The second is that, fallen from grace for some unknown reason, she was repudiated by her husband. Perhaps, emba-rrassed by misfortune, Akhe-naten attributed the death of his daughter to a punishment from Aten for the lack of male heirs, which the pharaoh would have ended up blaming on his wife. Others, however, believe that Nefertiti kept close to her husband and was the enigmatic regent Nefer-neferuaten. Archaeological findings regarding the confu-sing last years of Akhenaten seem to indicate that Nefertiti in fact died and that the regen-cy sometimes attributed to her actually corresponded to Meritaten, their daughter, who married Smenkhare, the brief successor of Akhenaten. The absence of references to Nefertiti in the last years of the pharaoh's reign has intri-gued generations of Egyptolo-gists, who do not rule out the possibility that the revenge of the priests of Amon extended to the queen's remains, and condemned her to the worst punishment imaginable: era-sing her name and making it disappear from history. The discoveries in the Valley of the Kings of tomb KV35 (by the Frenchman Victor

Valley of the Queens

Almost a mile southwest of the Valley of the Kings lies a place known as the Valley of the Queens, burial grounds with the remains of royal consorts of the Nineteenth and Twentieth Dynasties. The necropolis received its name because in it are located the tombs of Nefertari, the favorite wife of Ramesses II, and other queens of the Nineteenth Dynasty. However, the place had also been used by the previous dynasty to bury the young princes who died in infancy as well as some members of the nobility. Of the nearly one hundred graves discovered in the valley, few belong to queens. Its name in Egyptian is Ta Set Neferu, usually translated as "place of beauty." some Egyptologists, such as Christiane Desroches-Noblecourt and Christian Leblanc, have suggested that it should be translated as "place of the children."

The first queen laid to rest in this necropolis was Sitre, the wife of Ramesses I and mother of Seti I. Then followed Tuya, wife of Seti; Nefertari, the beloved wife of Ramesses II; the daughters of both, and other Ramesside queens. The next dynasty reverted to earlier burial practices, and designated the place as the final resting place of princes who died prematurely.

◄

TOMB OF NEFERTARI
Nefertari making an offering to the goddess Hathor, in one of the paintings in her beautiful tomb in the Valley of the Queens.

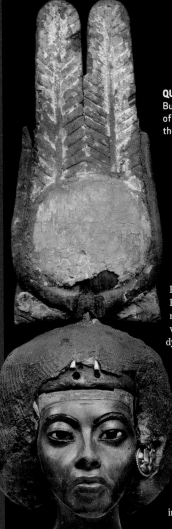

QUEEN TIYE
Bust of Tiye, wife of Amenhotep III and mother of Akhenaten and outstanding representative of the wives of the Seventeenth Dynasty.

Without Tombs

The whereabouts of the tombs of the queens of the Eighteenth Dynasty remains one of the big questions Egyptologists face. It is surprising that the great royal wives of Thutmose lacked their own mausoleum when compared to the consorts of previous and later dynasties. There are several expert opinions on this mystery. Briton Nicholas Reeves maintains that the queens' mausoleums must be in the Valley of the Kings, in rooms attached to the tombs of the pharaohs which have yet to be located. Meanwhile, his compatriot John Romer retains hope that the necropolis of these queens is in Medinet Habu, near Luxor.

With the exception of the Queen-Pharaoh Hatshepsut, whose tomb was built in the Valley of the Kings, no other tomb in the valley has been identified. Meanwhile, most of the mummies were found in the royal tombs of the Valley of the Kings or in nooks in the valley of Deir el-Bahri.

Aesthetic Ideals

In 1912, in the workshop of the sculptor Thutmose in Tell-el-Amarna, the German archaeologist Ludwig Borchardt discovered the famous multi-colored bust of Nefertiti. Comparison with the faces of other Egyptian sculptures led Egyptologists to assert that the face of the beautiful Nefertiti was idealized. A recent study using computed tomography has confirmed this by discovering a face inside the sculpture that is refined, but with different facial features. Thus the face of Nefertiti portrays the aesthetic ideals of the Amarna period, rather than reality.

Loret in 1889) and KV55 (by the Englishman Edward R. Ayrton in 1907) fueled new hopes about the whereabouts of Nefertiti and Akhenaten. However, it has taken over a hundred years to discover the identity of the mummies found in the tombs. In 2010, archaeologist Zahi Hawass, accompanied by a multidisciplinary scientific team, reported that, thanks to DNA testing, it could be concluded that the mummy of tomb KV35 known as the "Old Lady" was Queen Tiye, and that of the "Young Lady" who accompanied her was one of her daughters and the mother of Pharaoh Tutankhamun, though her identity was unknown. He also stated that the skeleton found inside a coffin in the tomb KV55 was the son of Tiye and Tutankhamun's father, and went as far as to put forth that it might be Pharaoh Akhenaten. Lastly, he refuted the idea that the "Young Lady" was, as was claimed by British Egyptologist Joann Fletcher, the mummy of Nefertiti. And so the whereabouts of the most beautiful of Egyptian queens remains a mystery.

Identification of Mummies

Establishing the identity of a person deceased thousands of years ago requires a multidisciplinary process that combines information from historical texts, archaeological findings, anthropology, and technological advances in medicine.

X-rays

The use of X-rays as tool to assist with the identification of mummies is ranked in second place since the advent of computed tomography with its advanced features. Nevertheless, x-ray is still a common initial technique, and it is especially useful in locating bony lesions or skeletal malformations which identify a character.

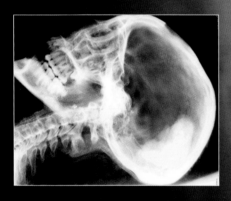

DENTAL AGE DETERMINATION
X-ray of skull (*top*) and the mummy of the "Young Lady," found in tomb KV35, which British Egyptologist Joann Fletcher wrongly attributed to Nefertiti in 2003. The skull image plates serve to determine the person's age by the teeth and cranial joints. In this case, it was found that the "Young Lady," the mother of Tutankhamen, was about 25 years old when she died.

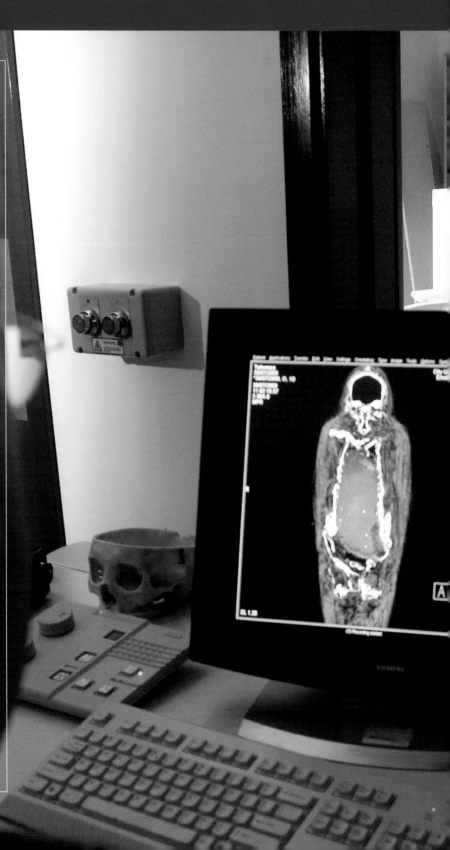

Arcaheological Support

The lists of the kings of Ancient Egypt that have discovered (the royal lists of Karnak and Abydos – shown in the image to the left – and in Saqqara, the Palermo Stone, and the Turin Royal Canon) are essential references for the identification of mummies. The priest Manetho's Aegyptiaca (second century BCE), a historical record with biographies of the great pharaohs, rescued by later historians, also provides valuable information.

DNA Revelations

DNA identification tests have revolutionized the world of Egyptology. Not only have they uncovered the identity of unknown mummies, as was the case with Akhenaten and Queen Tiye (his mother), but they also confirmed the practice of royal incest during the Eighteenth Dynasty. Thanks to DNA testing, it has been discovered that the mother of Tutankhamen was one of Akhenaten's five sisters, with whom Akhenaten had an incestuous relationship.

1 NO CONTAMINATION
After selecting the mummy to be researched, geneticists take necessary protective measures to avoid contaminating it with traces of their own DNA.

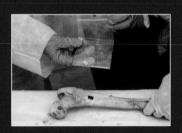

2 TAKING SAMPLES
Tissue samples are taken from different parts of the body of the mummy, especially the interior of the bones, the most useful due to being the most protected from outside contamination.

3 ANALYSIS
In the laboratory, the genetic composition of the tissue sample is analyzed. After isolating the chromosomes, the gender is established and the markers and alleles are located in the gene sequences.

4 MATCHES
Alleles are compared in areas with high variability for possible progenitors. If there are matches in at least eight of these segments, the paternal or maternal relationship is confirmed.

Tomography

Computed tomography is very valuable to Egyptologists because it allows for the analysis of mummified bodies without invasive practices. This imaging system, which provides three-dimensional high-resolution images, can detect anomalies with high accuracy. This facilitates the identification of a character by contrasting the result of the scan with available biographical data. Thereby, as Egyptologist Zahi Hawass explains in his work regarding the identification of Tutankhumen's relatives, a tomography of the purported skeleton of Akhenaten revealed that he had osteoarthritis, a condition that appears in old age. The finding invalidated the previous belief that the individual died aged 25 and, together with the results of the DNA testing, affirmed that the heretic pharaoh was the father of Tutankhamen.

What Mysteries Surround the Great Sphinx?

Who built it, when, and why are the major questions posed by this colossal monument with a lion's body and human head that has guarded the Giza necropolis for thousands of years.

The Great Sphinx of Giza is the embodiment of mystery. At first glance it seems to be the guardian of the pharaonic necropolis of Giza. Its impressive form with the body of a lion and a human head hide traces of the distant past that no one has yet been able to clarify with scientific facts. It was surprisingly ignored in the historical records of the Old Empire, during which, according to Egyptologists, it was sculpted. Thus, its age has always been a mystery. While experts generally agree that it was created during the Fourth Dynasty, various other theories have been formulated, based on the erosion of the monument, which attribute an age to the Great Sphinx ranging from 9,000 to 15,000 years old. However, the research of

eminent geologists, archaeologists, and Egyptologists have refuted those claims still defended by Americans John Anthony West (Egyptologist and esoteric author), as well as geophysicist Robert M. Schoch. Furthermore, the fact that for almost 3,100 of its 4,500 years of existence it has been covered by desert sand up to the neck, and even completely in some periods, the effects of erosion on the structure cannot be accurately measured.

HIDDEN TREASURES

It seems clear that the purpose of the Great Sphinx is to protect a sacred site, such as the tombs of the first pharaohs who during their lifetimes rose to the rank of gods. However, the fact that it faces east, directly toward the sunrise during the March and September equinoxes, has added cosmic significance to the enormous and

enigmatic statue. Beginning with the Roman historian Pliny (first century BCE), there have been echoes of rumors that hidden inside the Sphinx was the tomb of King Horemheb (or Harmais). Fantasies about treasures hidden beneath this giant structure have endured to this day.

In fact, geological surveys were carried out to search for hidden rooms or unknown crypts throughout the entire Giza plateau, particularly around the Sphinx. Through this research, several "anomalies" have been identified underground near the monument. In 1935, at the foot of the Pyramid of Khafra, a burial ground was located which included the crypt called the "Pit of Osiris." And yet, the passageways located and explored around the Great Sphinx have not led to any graves nor hidden rooms full of treasures.

DURABLE LIMESTONE
The head of the Sphinx is carved into a stronger limestone than that making up the layers that form the lion's body.

enigmas

WAS THE GREAT SPHINX AN OBJECT OF RELIGIOUS WORSHIP?

When the Great Sphinx was rediscovered during the New Kingdom after centuries of neglect, Thutmose IV identified it with the god Horemakhet ("Horus in the horizon, perfect God, the living God, ruler of eternity, lord of the desert") and established its worship. According to the inscriptions on the stele placed at the foot of the monument, the then Prince Thutmose went hunting in the desert. After an exhausting day, sleep overcame him and he dozed off under the head of the Great Sphinx. As he slept, he dreamed that the sculpture came to life and promised to make him master of Egypt if he rescued it from the sand. Thutmose did his part – he even dedicated a new temple to it – and the Great Sphinx did its part. In the New Kingdom the colossal monument became a location for pilgrimages by the Egyptian people. This custom prevailed until the fourth century BCE when the Roman Emperor Theodosius banned pagan cults.

Profile of Khafra

The identity of the face of the Great Sphinx is also clouded by mystery. Most Egyptologists agree that it corresponds to the Pharaoh Khafra, under whose reign it was most likely built. The obvious integration of the Great Sphinx into the Giza burial site, as well as subsequent archaeological findings, seem to support that idea. However, the comparisons made by archaeologist Mark Lehner between the face of the Sphinx and the statues of Pharaoh Khafra have not been satisfactory. So the mystery lingers, even though the Dream Stele of Thutmose IV also maintains that the construction of the colossal monument was undertaken by this pharaoh of the Fourth Dynasty.

Did They Marry Their Sisters?

Though it has not been shown to be practiced in all the dynasties, pharaohs from the New Kingdom had incestuous relationships with their sisters and daughters in order to keep the supreme power among their family lineage.

The pharaoh was considered God on Earth, the reincarnation of Osiris, the God who conquered death thanks to his sister and wife Isis, with whom he conceived Horus. Imitating the founding gods of Egypt, their heirs on Earth married their blood relations. Succession to the throne was established in such a way that the women of the royal family were the custodians of the rights to the throne, and so the heir had to marry one of the daughters of the great royal wife of his father. In this way they maintained the sacred character of the pharaoh's lineage, the source of their absolute power. Overall, carnal relationships between members of the royal family were an infrequent practice, confined to particular times in Ancient Egypt, essentially to the New Kingdom and the Ptolemaic period.

During the Second Intermediate Period, at the end of the Seventeenth Theban dynasty, Ahhotep I married her eldest brother Seqenenre Tao. Their son, Ahmose I, who threw out the Hyksos and founded the Eighteenth Dynasty of the New Kingdom, followed the example of his parents and also married several of his sisters. One of them, Ahmose-Nefertari, became his "Great Royal Wife and Mistress of The Two Lands," and was promoted to "God's Wife," a title passed from mother to daughter which accredited their royal origin, the purity of their blood, and the legitimacy of their ancestry.

AMENHOTEP I AND AHMOSE-MERITAMON
Marriage Between Siblings
Problems due to consanguinity became obvious during his reign. None of their offspring reached adult age.

RAMESSES II AND BINTANATH
Marriage Between Father And Daughter
Meritamon, Bintanath and Nebettawy were all great royal wives of their father. Henuttawy, another daughter, was a secondary wife. He had children with most of them.

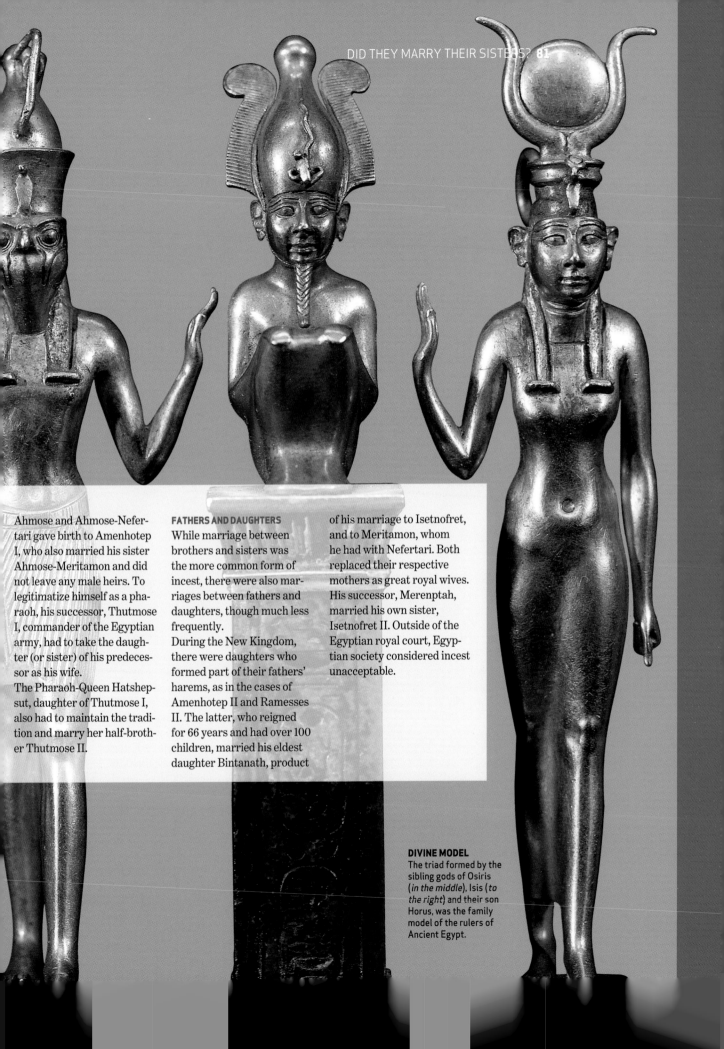

Ahmose and Ahmose-Nefertari gave birth to Amenhotep I, who also married his sister Ahmose-Meritamon and did not leave any male heirs. To legitimatize himself as a pharaoh, his successor, Thutmose I, commander of the Egyptian army, had to take the daughter (or sister) of his predecessor as his wife.

The Pharaoh-Queen Hatshepsut, daughter of Thutmose I, also had to maintain the tradition and marry her half-brother Thutmose II.

FATHERS AND DAUGHTERS

While marriage between brothers and sisters was the more common form of incest, there were also marriages between fathers and daughters, though much less frequently.

During the New Kingdom, there were daughters who formed part of their fathers' harems, as in the cases of Amenhotep II and Ramesses II. The latter, who reigned for 66 years and had over 100 children, married his eldest daughter Bintanath, product of his marriage to Isetnofret, and to Meritamon, whom he had with Nefertari. Both replaced their respective mothers as great royal wives. His successor, Merenptah, married his own sister, Isetnofret II. Outside of the Egyptian royal court, Egyptian society considered incest unacceptable.

DIVINE MODEL
The triad formed by the sibling gods of Osiris (*in the middle*), Isis (*to the right*) and their son Horus, was the family model of the rulers of Ancient Egypt.

How Did Cleopatra Die?

Cleopatra VII was heir of the Ptolemaic Greek Dynasty and a symbol of Egyptian culture. She was Ancient Egypt's last hope for recovering their influence in a world dominated by Roman rule.

Born into the Ptolemaic dynasty, which originated in Macedonia and was characterized by conspiracies and murders between relatives, the last queen of Ancient Egypt learned how to nimbly maneuver through the intricacies of politics. Daughter of Ptolemy XII Neos Dionysos and his sister Cleopatra V Tryphaena, Cleopatra VII was named co-regent at 14 years old, alongside her brother Ptolemy XIII, who was 10. Upon the death of her father in 51 BCE she had to marry. Cleopatra called herself "Goddess Lover of Her Father" and "Lady of the Two Lands," in order to reaffirm her power as pharaoh and win public favor. This she gained quickly, as she was the first of the Ptolemaics to speak the Egyptian language, unlike her ancestors, who had kept their Greek culture and language.

The alleged beauty of the young queen Cleopatra aroused the desire of the two most powerful men of the age, the Roman generals Julius Caesar and Mark Antony. With Julius Caesar, who became her lover, she had a son, Ptolemy VI, also known as Caesarion. Then she married Mark Antony and gave birth to twins. However, despite her romantic bond with these distinguished generals, Cleopatra aimed to preserve the independence of Egypt and defied the power of Rome, represented in the form of Octavian, Mark Antony's rival.

THE LAST QUEEN

Myth, legend and propaganda intermix when talking about the last, energetic, and fascinating queen of Ancient Egypt. In his *Life of Antony*, the Greek historian and biographer Plutarch (46–119 CE) described Cleopatra as a woman of conventional beauty, but as possessing great powers of speech, capable of dazzling her listeners with the persuasion of her words. And he added: "She also produced pleasure with the tone of her voice. And her tongue was an instrument of many strings. She could easily switch from one language to another, and few were the barbarians she used an interpreter to communicate with."

The death of Cleopatra, which took place during the year 30 BCE, ended 3000 years of Pharaonic Egyptian history. Defeat in the naval battle of Actium (31 BCE) left Egypt open for Octavian to annex it to Rome. To avoid the humiliation of defeat, Mark Antony killed himself. Later, far from her husband, tradition has it that Cleopatra let herself be bitten by an asp, hidden in a basket of figs; though it is also speculated that she could have been killed by poison, ingested on the orders of the victorious Octavian.

enigmas

WHERE IS CLEOPATRA'S TOMB?

Queen Cleopatra's body has never been discovered. A team of Dominican-Egyptian archaeologists thought that the mystery was solved in 2008 when they identified the area of Taposiris Magna, a site 30 miles (48 km) to the west of Alexandria, as the place of her burial, alongside the tombstone of Mark Antony. However, the body still has not been discovered.

BITE
Pictorial rendition of Cleopatra's suicide.

Mystery

Not even Plutarch, the first to write of the death of Cleopatra, had the courage to confirm that the last queen of Egypt had died as he described. After saying that she had committed suicide and that an asp had injected her with its poison, and adding that there were other opinions about how it had been administered, such as through a hollow knife, he concluded: "That is how they say it happened." In reality, how it happened is not known. Historians do not rule out the idea that Cleopatra was murdered and that Octavian spread a story designed to beautify her death and calm her supporters. Even though the specifics remain unresolved, experts agree that poison was the fatal agent.

DISCREDITING CAMPAIGN
After the death of Cleopatra, Octavian tried to discredit her. One example is this Roman tetradrachm with a profile of the queen that puts her beauty into question.

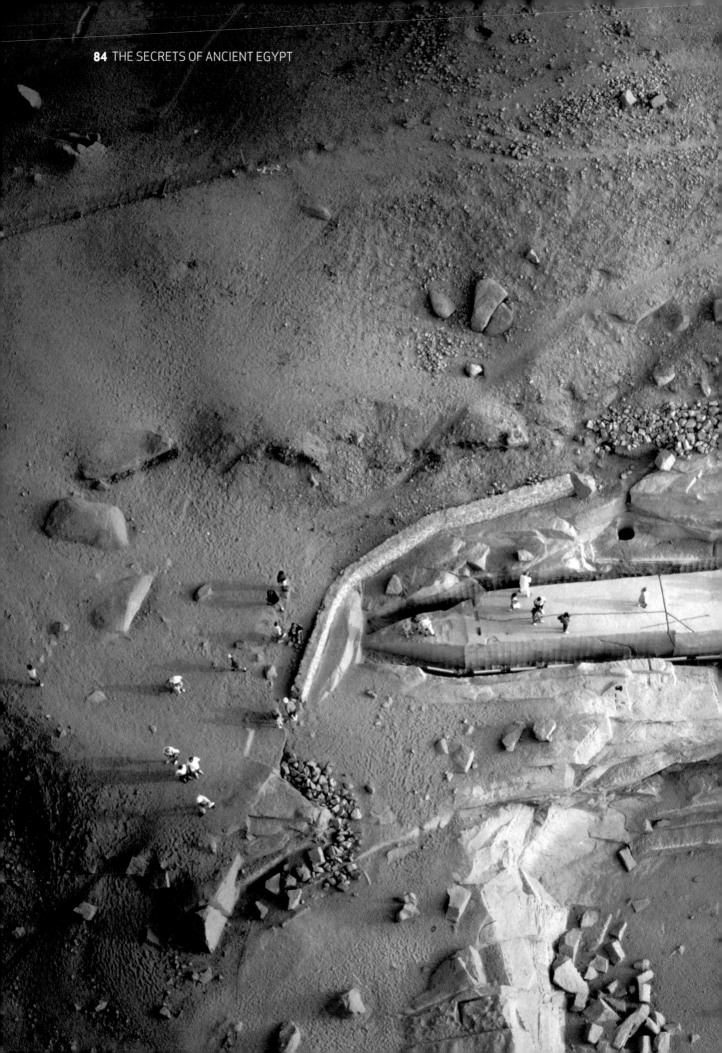

DISAGREEMENT
It is believed that the enormous unfinished obelisk of Aswan, 138 ft
(42 m) long, was commissioned by the Pharaoh-Queen Hatshepsut of
the Eighteenth Dynasty, the woman who was in power for the longest
amount of time in Ancient Egypt. Others, however, believe it was commissioned by her coregent Thutmose III and that its purpose was to
accompany the obelisk from Karnak, now located in St. John Lateran
square in Rome.

Alternative Hypotheses

Who Set Fire to the Library of Alexandria?

Rumors regarding the destruction of the Library of Alexandria – founded by the first Pharaohs of the Ptolemaic dynasty – still persist today. With close to a million manuscripts, open to the public and to scholars from all over the Mediterranean, it was considered to be one of the wonders of the Ancient World. One day it disappeared in flames, after being set on fire by the orders of a Roman leader – there is no consensus on which one. It may have been Julius Caesar (48 BCE), Aurelian (273 CE), emperor Diocletian (297 CE) or, some say, the bishop Theophilus, under Theodosius I (391 CE). Yet other versions name the caliph Umar (581–644 CE), saying he distributed the library's manuscripts amongst bath houses to use them to feed the fires used to heat the cauldrons.

Was Princess Beketaten the Mother of Tutankhamun?

After DNA tests carried out on the mummies, it was discovered that Tutankhamun's mother was the sister of his father, Akhenaten, with whom he had an incestuous relationship. Now we might ask: Which of Akhenaten's sisters was it? Sitamun, Iset, Henuttaneb, Nebetiah, or Beketaten? Thus far, and in accordance with the biographical data collected regarding the princesses, it seems that Beketaten might be the most probable candidate. The youngest daughter of Amenhotep III and Queen Tiye, she stayed with her mother at Thebes until her mother's death. The fact that her mummy was placed next to that of queen Tiye in the KV35 tomb would not have been an accident. The experts do not dismiss the fact that the young woman, who appeared to have died violently, was originally buried next to her parent, with whom she had been very close.

ALEXANDRIAN TREASURE
Engraving that illustrates the inside of the celebrated Egyptian library.

Who Was the First Female Pharaoh?

At the moment, two individuals vie for this title: Nitocris and Sobekneferu. According to Manetho (third century BCE), the author of the most extensive and detailed royal chronologies of Ancient Egypt, the last sovereign of the Sixth Dynasty of the Old Kingdom of Egypt was a woman called Nitocris (in Greek). He described her as "more brave than all the men of her time, and the most beautiful of all the women, with beautiful skin and red cheeks," and he attributed the construction of the Pyramid of Menkaure to her. However, in the absence of other more reliable records, Egyptologists believe that she was actually a myth. Alternatively, Sobekneferu actually appears in the royal lists of Saqqara and Abydos. She was the daughter of the Pharaoh Amenemhat III and the last sovereign of the Middle Kingdom of Egypt in the eighteenth century BCE.

When Did the Exodus of the Jews Occur?

The date when the Jews left Egypt after God sent the 10 plagues to the country of the pharaohs, as per the Biblical record, remains a mystery. Though there are various theories, most agree that the people of Israel set out on their journey to the Promised Land during the New Kingdom, at the time of the Nineteenth Dynasty. One theory connects the departure of the Hebrews with Akhenaten, who they even associate with Moses, though science has recently refuted this last claim, which would have meant that the famous and revolutionary pharaoh left his native Egypt. Another theory is that it occurred during the rein of Merneptah, the successor of the all-powerful Ramesses II, because in a stele initialed by him there is an inscription about the people of Ysyriar, which some Egyptologists believe – though there is no further proof of it – to be the first historical reference to the people of Israel. This opinion seems to be supported by the contemptuous statement inscribed upon the monument: "Ysyriar is laid waste. His seed is not."

MOSES
The liberator of the people of Israel was a prince of Egypt.

Alternative Hypotheses

Were the Builders of Thutmose I's Tomb Executed?

When Howard Carter excavated the KV20 tomb in 1904 in the Valley of the Kings, he uncovered the following inscription: "No one heard or saw anything." Such an enigmatic text soon aroused speculations regarding its meaning. Seeing the design of the tomb, with a strange curve towards the right inside the mountain ending in the burial chamber, he immediately attributed a macabre meaning to it. A simple analysis of the tomb demonstrates that the builder, the celebrated architect Ineni, tried to make it difficult to access the tomb, so as to hide it. In fact, the location and the construction of the mausoleum were considered to have been a state decision. Because of all this, Carter was led to conclude that the workers that had participated in the construction were executed afterward. Other researchers, however, believe that this human sacrifice wouldn't make sense. Firstly, the Deir el-Medina guild of artisans already existed, dedicated to the excavation of the tombs in the Theban cemetery, and secondly, it was founded by Thutmose I himself, who was later buried at this site – though it was repurposed by his daughter Hatshepsut. Given these factors, it is probable that these words specifically alluded to the existence of this very community of artisans, which lived on the margins of Egyptian society. The authorities tried to keep the workers and artisans quiet about the location and magnificence of the tombs.

THUTMOSE I
He was the first Pharaoh to have his hypogeum built in the Valley of the Kings.

Does the Great Sphinx Hide Treasures from Atlantis?

Some believe that underneath the sands of the Great Sphinx of Giza, archives from the Atlantean civilization were hidden away. The North American seer Edgar Cayce (1877–1945) claimed in his works that the treasure of the archives of Atlantis was buried in a chamber underneath the Sphinx in order to avoid the danger of flooding. Cayce was known as the "sleeping prophet" and believed in the reincarnation of souls from Atlantis. His theories had a large audience due to his visions of the original Atlantis, an island purported to be at the latitude of the Pillars of Hercules and larger than Libya and Asia together. Also described by the Greek philosopher Plato in Critias and Timaeus, which later disappeared under the sea. Although Cayce's theories fueled beliefs about the Great Sphinx as a product of a pre-Egyptian civilization 8,000 to 12,500 years old, nobody has been able to find access to the passage leading to the hidden treasure of Atlantis.

Was There a Labyrinth Between the Pyramids?

In his monumental *History*, Herodotus echoed the legend of the existence of an Egyptian labyrinth which he considered indescribable. Despite defining it in this way, he also spoke in minute detail about what he had seen – which was a place made up of streets, crossroads, and subterranean rooms decorated with multicolored reliefs, from which pyramids rose, emerging from a gigantic lake. Other historians, such as the Greek Strabo and the Roman Pliny the Elder, also talked about the labyrinth, which they said could be visited in the second century. Since then, no one has been able to locate such a wonder of wonders.

Did the Pharaohs Build the First Suez Canal?

It is said that during the Ptolemaic dynasty an attempt to build a canal joining the Mediterranean Sea and the Red Sea was undertaken. In the end, the pharaohs' project did not proceed, because of fears that it would cause a large flood. However, before that time pharaohs had already planned to build a canal between the Red Sea and the Nile River. Greek sources even mention Senusret I as being responsible for the idea, although it is said that in reality it was an overland route, through which ships could be transported in pieces and then be rebuilt on the shores of the Red Sea.

Did the Sphinx Once Have a Lion's Head?

This is the opinion of two British scholars, the geologist Colin Reader and the architectural historian Jonathan Foyle, who second the theory that the esoteric Alsatian Rene Schwaller de Lubicz (1887–1961) promoted for several decades. Like other researchers, they base their Hypotheses on the disproportionate ratio of the head of the Sphinx with the rest of its body. Additionally, they believe that it could have been modified later in order to model the face of the Pharaoh Khafra, and that prior to that it had the appearance of a lion. Aside from the similarity that the nemes – the headdress of a Pharaoh – has with a lion's mane, the scholars base their theory on the degree of erosion that the Sphinx shows. In this way, they agree with the theories of the geophysicist Robert M. Schoch, who maintains that the Great Sphinx might be between 9,000 and 15,000 years old.

EGYPTIAN SHIP
Egypt maintained active maritime trade between Asia Minor and the Red Sea.

To See and Visit

▼ OTHER PLACES OF INTEREST

THE GIZA SPHINX
CAIRO, EGYPT

The Great Sphinx of Giza, over 160 ft (48 m) long and almost 65 ft tall and made of limestone, is a continuing enigma. Research performed by a Japanese university recently uncovered a series of passages around it. Visitors can see the Sphinx along with the other monuments in Giza.

MIT RAHINA
EGYPT

In this small town, visitors can see the ruins of Memphis, the capital of Ancient Egypt. An open-air museum has been set up here, allowing visitors to walk among the remains that give hints of the splendor the city once had. Highlights include monumental statues, sphinxes, and archaeological remnants of palaces and temples.

MONUMENTS BY RAMESSES II
ABU SIMBEL, EGYPT

Cut from the rocks in southern Egypt, on the west bank of Lake Nasser, they form part of the Open Air Museum of Nubia and Aswan. These colossal twin temples were built by Ramesses II around 1274 BCE. and dedicated to his and his wife, Nefertaris, worship. They are some of the best-preserved monuments in Egypt.

UNIVERSITY OF PENNSYLVANIA MUSEUM OF ARCHAEOLOGY AND ANTHROPOLOGY
PHILDELPHIA

The collection of mummies, statues, and bas-reliefs in this institution, which includes over 42,000 objects of Egyptian art, is considered one of the best in the world. Among its treasures, an enormous granite sphinx of Ramses II from around 1200 BCE stands out.

Memphis

SAQQARA
This is the site of one of the largest necropolises in Egypt and the most important in the ancient capital of Memphis. It was used for more than 3000 years, from the First Egyptian Dynasty until the arrival of Christianity. Various funerary monuments are found here, including 17 pyramids for pharaohs, royal tombs in subterranean chambers and mausoleums for dignitaries and nobles.

ZOSER FUNERARY COMPLEX
Around 20 mi (32 km) from Cairo visitors can access this complex in Saqqara, including the well-known Step Pyramid of Zoser, constructed by Imhotep, the first architect known to history. It is believed that this pyramid, 450 ft (137 m) long and 390 ft (118 m) wide, is the first work ever built entirely of stone. The complex also contains the remains of various temples, chapels, trenches, and an intricate system of passageways where sarcophagi have been found.

SERAPEUM
The sacred Bulls of Apis were the most venerated and sacred animals in Egypt. This subterranean necropolis where these sacred bulls were buried in stone sarcophagi (granite or basalt) after embalming is found to the north of Saqqara. The mummy of a son of Ramesses II (who died around 1213 BCE) who chose to be buried with the sacred bulls was also found here.

Amarna

Akhenaten stripped Thebes of its status as the capital city and raised a new city midway between Thebes and Memphis around the fourteenth century BCE. The city carried the name of Akhetaten, the "Horizon of Aten," and was built quickly. And as quickly as it bloomed, it was destroyed. Today some of its ruins, such as the unfinished tomb of the heretic pharaoh, can be visited.

METROPOLITAN MUSEUM OF ART
NEW YORK CITY
This museum has a large collection of Egyptian art exhibited in 40 galleries encompassing more than 26,000 objects running from Paleolithic to Roman times. Many of these objects were found through excavations performed by the Museum between 1906 and 1941.

CZARTORYSKI MUSEUM
KRAKOW, POLAND
This museum, which has belonged to a noble Polish family since its founding in 1796, has in its collection true gems such as a da Vinci, and a no less striking series of Egyptian mummies and sarcophagi of incalculable historical value.

ARCHAEOLOGICAL MUSEUM
FLORENCE, ITALY
After the Egyptian Museum in Turin, the Archaeological Museum in Florence has the second most important collection of Egyptian art in Italy. And with good reason: its collection was built around a central collection started by the Medicis and later increased in the eighteenth century through the institution's participation in various excavations. Today it houses an exhibition of more than 14,000 pieces, among which are statues dating to the reign of Amenhotep III (between 1388 and 1351 BCE), a carriage from the Eighteenth Dynasty, and a column from the Tomb of Seti (around 1270 BCE).

Glossary

ARISTOTLE An ancient Greek philosopher who lived from 384 to 322 BCE.

BEATIFIED In ancient Egyptian theology, one who is beatified has entered heaven or has made some celestial ascension.

EGYPTOLOGY The study of ancient Egypt and its history, artifacts, and antiquities.

EMBALMING The process of preserving the remains of the human body through alteration to slow the decomposing process, most often for funerals and burials.

EXCAVATING Digging or tunneling to uncover something buried in the ground.

FACADE A structure's front; sometimes referring to the front of a structure, or face, which has been specially modified.

FUNERARY Anything involving the process of funerals or commemoration of the dead.

HERODOTUS A Greek historian who allegedly witnessed the construction of pyramids in addition to many other events in history.

ISIS (AST) The ancient Egyptian goddess of nature, both sister and partner to the god Osiris.

KHUFU A pharaoh of ancient Egypt, the second pharoah of the Fourth Dynasty in the Old Kingdom period.

MAUSOLEUM A type of tomb, in which the dead are usually buried aboveground, with the coffin inside a large stone structure.

NECROPOLIS Any exceptionally large, intricate cemetery in ancient cities.

OLD KINGDOM The period in the third millenium BCE that marked the height of civilization in ancient Egypt.

RA The ancient Egyptian god of the sun.

ROSETTA STONE Found in 1799, a special stone with hieroglyphics on it used to translate ancient Egyptian hieroglyphics.

SARCOPHAGUS A coffin of stone, used in the ancient civilizations of Egypt, Rome, and Greece, often accompanied by statues and engravings.

SPHINX A mythical creature commemorated in the Great Sphinx statue of ancient Egypt. A sphinx had the body of a lion and, most often, a man's head, but it sometimes had the head of an eagle or ram.

SUBTERRANEAN Anything beneath the surface of the earth.

Further Reading

Creighton, Scott, and Rand Flem-Ath. *The Secret Chamber of Osiris: Lost Knowledge of the Sixteen Pyramids*. Rochester, VT: Bear & Company—Inner Traditions International, 2015.

Harrison, Paul. *The Curse of the Pharaoh's Tombs: Tales of the unexpected since the days of Tutankhamun*. Great Britain, UK: Pen and Sword Archaeology—Pen and Sword Books, LTD., 2017.

Heimlich, Rüdiger, and Wfaa El Saddik. *Protecting Pharaoh's Treasures: My Life in Egyptology*. New York, NY: The American University in Cairo Press, 2017.

Lehner, Mark. *The Complete Pyramids*. New York, NY: Thames and Hudson, 1997.

Pirelli, Rosanna. *The Queens of Ancient Egypt*. New York, NY: White Star Publishers, 2010.

Redford, Donald B. *From Slave to Pharaoh: The Black Experience of Ancient Egypt*. Baltimore, MD: Johns Hopkins University Press, 2006

Romer, John. *A History of Ancient Egypt: From the First Farmers to the Great Pyramid*. New York, NY: Thomas Dunne Books—St. Martin's Press, 2013.

Romer, John. *A History of Ancient Egypt Volume 2: From the Great Pyramid to the Fall of the Middle Kingdom*. United Kingdom: Thomas Dunne Books—St. Martin's Press, 2017.

Schoch, Robert M. *Pyramid Quest: Secrets of the Great Pyramid and the Dawn of Civilization*. New York, NY: Penguin Books, 2005.

Shoup III, John A. *The Nile: An Encyclopedia of Geography, History, and Culture*. Santa Barbara, CA: ABCE-CLIO—ABCE-CLIO, LLC., 2017.

Smith, Mark. *Following Osiris: Perspectives on the Osirian Afterlife from Four Millenia*. Oxford, UK: Oxford University Press, 2017.

Venit, Marjorie Susan. *Visualizing the Afterlife in the Tombs of Graeco-Roman Egypt*. New York, NY:Cambridge University Press, 2016.

Vischnak, Deborah. *Community and Identity in Ancient Egypt: The Old Kingdom Cemetery at Qubbet el-Hawa*. New York, NY: Cambridge University Press, 2015.

Wilkinson, Richard H. *Pharoah's Land and Beyond: Ancient Egypt and Its Neighbors*. New York, NY: Oxford University Press, 2017.

WEBSITES

Archaeology in Egypt

http://www.aeraweb.org/projects

The Ancient Egypt Research Associates (AERA) website provides detailed descriptions of the organization's archaeological findings, along with a list of their lectures and publications.

Mysteries of Egypt

http://www.historymuseum.ca/cmc/exhibitions/civil/egypt/egcivile.shtml

The Canadian Museum of Civilization offers a comprehensive look at life in ancient Egypt, providing insight into its government, religion, scientific discoveries, and details of typical daily routines.

The Theban Mapping Project

http://www.thebanmappingproject.com

The Theban Mapping Project features a large database of the archaeological sites that have been explored in Thebes.

Virtual Egyptian Museum

http://www.virtual-egyptian-museum.org

The Virtual Egyptian Museum features a collection of images of ancient Egyptian artifacts, many of which are no longer on view in museums. The website provides detailed descriptions and commentary on these artifacts, along with images of the artifacts from numerous perspectives.

Index